A TEENAGER SURVIVING DEPRESSION

Arrionna Wright-Cross

Copyright ©2025
All rights reserved. Written permission must be secured from the author to reproduce any part of the book.

Printed in the United States of America

ISBN: 979-8-3492-3697-6

10 9 8 7 6 5 4 3 2 1

EMPIRE PUBLISHING
www.empirebookpublishing.com

Dedication

To my father. For providing the punishments and the love that made me grow into the young woman I am today. Without my father, I would be lost. For my father, I live.

Table of Contents

Chapter 1 1
    5th Grade 1
Chapter 2 7
    Party Time 7
Chapter 3 19
    Celebration Day 19
Chapter 4 32
    Graduation 32
Chapter 5 50
    Bye-Bye Fifth Grade 50
Chapter 6 60
    Summer Vacation 60
Chapter 7 87
    Middle School 87
Chapter 8 92
    Is This Real 92
Chapter 9 100
    Am I Done Yet? 100
Chapter 10 107
    Spring Preserve 107

CHAPTER 11 117
    I Don't Know 117
CHAPTER 12 122
    Even Good Days Have to End 122
CHAPTER 13 126
    My Parents 126
CHAPTER 14 129
    I Survived 129
EPILOGUE 131

Depression. Suicide. Puberty. Growth. Four words that are so similar, yet so different. Four words that, to this day, I'm still learning. Four words that I wish I knew more about in different times of my life, but four words I'm glad I figured out.

Hello, my name is Arrionna Wright-Cross and this is how I survived *Depression*.

Chapter 1

5th Grade

Ah, 2017. Fifth grade year. My life was great, I had a lot of friends, well "friends" ... Anyways the fact is that I was very popular among the hallways of James B. McMillan, an elementary school right in the center of Summerlin, Las Vegas. Out of all the friends I had, I had two main friends. Lila and June. They were my besties. We hung out like almost every day, and had the same favorite foods and sports, so it was kind of destined for us to be best friends. I also had good grades, Great even. Eleven years old and not a problem in the world…well besides my peanut allergy but that wasn't anything too big in my opinion.

"Can you believe that we're going to be 6th graders in about a month!?" June said

"Well technically we're not sixth graders until September," said Lila.

Lila was the smart one out of our group. She was the one we looked to when we didn't know the meaning behind the big words that the art teacher made us use to describe paintings. Which by the way, most of those words she used were definitely made up, because there was no way that "philosophical" was a word; but I digress.

June was the funny, sarcastic one out of us. She was secretly really smart and didn't want anyone to know, but Liyah and I knew the truth and to us that's all that mattered.

"Okay whatever, the big objective is that we're going to be sixth graders soon!" I say laughing.

I never really thought about being in sixth grade before that day honestly. I watched YouTube videos of girls waking up at seven AM to get ready and do their makeup but that was it and even then that was still kind of mind-boggling to me. Seven AM??...I don't even get up at seven am for breakfast, so I couldn't imagine waking up at seven just to get ready for school, but what did I know? I was still a 5th grader.

"Well, are you guys ready for graduation or what?!" Lila sighed dramatically

"I mean duhhh! What color are we wearing?" asked June,

"Mmm, I was thinking pink—something bright and fun! What do you think, Arri?" exclaims Lila.

"Wait, why don't we go with an ocean like blue? It'll look so good on us." said June.

As Lila and June chatter animatedly about the possibilities, I found myself somewhat adrift, lost in my own thoughts. I was still stuck on the question Lila had posed just moments before. Was I truly ready for graduation?

If you were talking about being prepared to learn how to open a locker—something I had already practiced multiple times—and facing the challenge of juggling six different classes each day, then sure, I was more than ready. I could handle those without a problem. But if the question leaned more toward whether I was emotionally prepared to say goodbye to the comforts of my current life and step into a future with uncertainty and tons of responsibility, well, that was a different story altogether.

I sat there, grappling with feelings of excitement and anxiety. Graduation represented a significant transition—a pivotal moment that meant closing one chapter of my life while simultaneously opening another.

Would I be ready when the time came? Or would I find myself yearning for the safety of what I already knew? That question sat with me until June's voice knocked me back into reality.

"Lila, you're way too obsessed with the color pink," June laughed, shaking her head

"Mmm, I totally agree!" I chimed in.

"Soo, what's wrong with that? I mean, it is a fabulous color!" Lila yells

"So, we're actually going to wear big, fluffy pink princess dresses to graduate? That sounds awesome!" June says sarcastically.

"I'm pretty sure they won't be big princess dresses, June," I added in.

"Obviously! But come on, it would make for some epic graduation photos!" Lila counters playfully.

"It's okay; we'll figure it all out tonight! My mom is here, so I'll call you guys later so we can talk about all the details more! Bye!" I said.

"Okay, bye Arri, get home safe!" my friends say.

I love talking about things with Lila and June. It always ends in someone laughing or smiling. We would do anything to make sure each other was happy. Well.. not anything. I definitely wouldn't trade my last chocolate chip little bite for one of their apple slices and I wasn't sure If I was going to match in pink dresses with them either.

Hey hey, I'm not contradicting myself—- it wouldn't be by my choice. I mean I obviously want to, but I knew my dad had something special planned for my graduation and I don't think it involves the color pink.

See, my dad is a spontaneous person. One moment we could all be relaxing in the house watching tv and next you know we're outside having a backflip competition created by my dad. So, I knew I wouldn't know what I was doing till the weekend of graduation... literally.

Later on that night, Lila called us, her voice brimming with excitement as she couldn't wait to show off her new dress that her mom had brought her. It wasn't officially her graduation dress yet since we still had some time, but she absolutely adored it and judging by the color choice, it seemed to confirm the unofficial hue for graduation festivities—pink.

Now, it was time for me to muster up all my persuasive skills to convince my dad to buy me a pink dress as well. I mean, it shouldn't be too hard... hopefully.

The week that followed was surprisingly easygoing and filled with anticipation. We dove right into planning for the end-of-the-year celebration party, which was shaping up to be the highlight of our school year. Oh wait, okay let me explain what the famous "Celebration Party" is.

You see, about a month before graduation, each student receives a colored card with the word "Celebration" boldly printed on it. Oh no, don't miscalculate, This card was not just a mere piece of paper; it held significant power.

If you lost all your letters on your celebration card, the consequences were dire—you would have to spend the party time of the celebration confined to the dreaded detention room, missing out on all the fun and festivities like you were locked up in a prison with a singular window to watch the world go on without you slowing forgetting your existence... okay maybe not that dramatic, but trust me, nobody wanted to end up there.

The detention room was in Mrs. H's classroom—an infamous place among every 5th grader at James B McMillian. Her classroom was known for its strict atmosphere, filled with walls plastered with rules, and an incessant ticking clock that seemed to mock those who found themselves trapped within those four walls. It was the last place anyone wanted to be during a celebration meant for laughter, games, fun and memories. The thought of being stuck there while everyone else enjoyed themselves was enough to make anyone double-check their celebration card, doing everything in their power to keep those precious letters and being on their best behavior.

There were four, 5th grade teachers at my school. My teacher, Ms. G, had the movie room. If you wanted to just relax or take a nap during the celebration you would go there (that's where the kids who didn't really like to talk would go). Which hey, I don't blame them, being a 5th grader was already hard enough why add unnecessary talking on a free calm day?

The teacher next to her, Mrs. V, was the "board game room". She had all the board games you could think of. Even the game of life!! Which, thinking back on it, I'm not sure why 5th graders were playing the game of life; but that's a different story. The teacher across the hall on the left was Ms. L room. Her room was the "party" room. Where we could dance and sing all celebration if we choose to. Sounds like paradise huh?

That's why for the next three and a half weeks everyone was on their best behavior. Helping out our teachers every chance we got, turning in their work early and even lining up in a quiet and perfect line for lunch.. Which for us 5th graders was really hard. Especially the quiet part, but we all took pride in it because the party was definitely gonna be worth it.

Chapter 2

Party Time

Ring Ring

"Heyyy guysss!" Liyah exclaims excitedly as Jay and I join the group call. Her voice brimming with enthusiasm "Should we all get matching outfits for the party? I mean, wouldn't that be so fun?"

"Mhm yeah, why not? What were you thinking of matching with, Lila?" I ask her, curious to hear her creative ideas.

"Well, I was thinking that tutu's would be absolutely adorable! She exclaimed.

I think our confused faces along with the awkward silence answered how June and I felt about that idea for us, because Lila quickly tried to explain her idea.

 Picture this: us prancing around in fluffy, colorful skirts, topped off with some glow-in-the-dark sticks made into bracelets and necklaces?? It would definitely turn heads and make a serious fashion statement,"

"Uh... no," June interjects

June has never been a fan of anything remotely girly. Well, not necessarily "girly" in the traditional sense. She does have a special fondness for bright rainbows and whimsical unicorns. She even cherishes butterflies, believing they are indeed the most beautiful creatures on

Earth. But when it comes to wearing a tutu? That's where she draws a firm line.

"Ugh... Arri?" Lila says, looking at me for support.

I chuckle a bit, trying to balance between Lila's enthusiasm and June's reluctance.

"Well, I'm honestly okay with anything! I think matching outfits could be a cute idea!" I say, attempting to straddle the fence between the two of them, hoping to find some middle ground.

"Okay, you two have fun because there is absolutely no way whatsoever that I will ever get into a tutu! I'll wear the glow-in-the-dark sticks, though—only if they come in blue or purple, of course!" June insists, crossing her arms.

We all burst into laughter as we agree that, in the end, we'll settle for just the glow-in-the-dark sticks. It's definitely a more appealing compromise for June and we don't have to beg our parents for money, which always ends up with us doing some form of a chore before we can fully convince them of their remittance anyway. We continue chatting, exchanging opinions and jokes, our excitement for the upcoming party growing as we plan the little details.

Before we know it, the hours slip away, and the conversation drifts into playful teasing and reminiscing old memories.

"Wow guys, we're really graduating soon." sighed Lila

"I know, isn't it crazy, " I responded.

"Yeah yeah. You know what's crazy? The fact that it's almost 8:30 and we're still up, its about my bedtime." June said

"Okay June you're right." Laughed Lila.

We reluctantly said our goodnights, promising to touch base tomorrow about more party details. As I hang up, I can't help but smile, already looking forward to the fun ahead.

"Good morning my love." my mother said waking me up the next morning.

"Good morning."

"Breakfast is at the table, hot and ready wherever you want to get to that."

"Okay, thank you mom." I replied

With the days only getting closer to graduation and my nerves only getting higher, I tried to focus on the party. Graduation was in two weeks and the party was in a week and a half, so I took it one thing at a time…. Still not hearing anything from my dad I assumed pink was not going to be an option. All the good pink dresses were already sold out the week before, which wasn't a surprise. Every eleven-year-old 5th grader dreamed of graduating in a pink dress... Well, almost every 5th grader.

Was it weird that I didn't share that same excitement? Not that I outright didn't want to; it was more that I didn't feel passionate about it. If I had to wear a pink dress, I wouldn't mind, but it wasn't something I would automatically choose. You know how it is—everyone seems to have their own little vision for this big moment, and mine was different.

I always pictured myself standing proudly on that stage in something cute and simple yet still special. Maybe a soft pastel color or a fun pattern that reflected my personality. Something that said, "This is Arri," and made me feel like I was truly celebrating the end of an era. But none of that seemed to matter right now. All around me, my friends were buzzing with excitement about the pink theme. They were sharing ideas, sending pictures of pink dresses they loved, and talking about how we would all match perfectly. It made sense that they adored the idea; pink was such a fun, cheerful color that echoed the spirit of our elementary school days. I knew joining in on the pink dress bandwagon would bring us all together and make the celebration feel even more special. So, even though I had my own preferences swirling in my mind, if pink was what my friends wanted to do, then that's what I'd embrace too.

"Hey mom, can you take me to the store?"

"Yeah, as soon as I'm done with work. What are you trying to get from there?" my mom questions

"Well Liyah, Jay and I were thinking about wearing glow in the dark bows for the celebration party."

"Oh that's a nice idea, yeah I have no problem taking you."

"Okay thank you."

My mom wasn't really the dressing up type. She preferred to keep it casual and simple, T-shirt and jeans paired with comfortable sneakers. It was a style that suited her well, perfectly reflecting her laid-back personality. But me on the other hand? She was fully aware that fashion was everything to me, especially during school. I made it a point to lay out my clothes and shoes the night before school, meticulously ensuring everything was ironed, properly folded, and dry cleaned to the touch; otherwise, the whole outfit would be a no-go. The right bow was just as important.

"So what kind of bows are you guys looking for, white? Black? Pink?" my mom asked, her eyes scanning the horizon as if searching for clues in the fashion wilderness.

"I think we're all going with baby pink to coordinate with our graduation dresses," I responded.

"Okay, I think Burlington might have some good options," she suggested.

"When I was there last week for you and your sister's summer clothes, I noticed they had a pretty decent accessory section. We can check that out and see what they have."

"Okay, that sounds perfect!" I exclaimed, feeling a rush of excitement over the potential treasures that awaited us.

When we finally arrived at Burlington, we were greeted by the vibrant atmosphere of the store, which buzzed with shoppers and chatter. We immediately spotted the accessories sign in big, bold white letters not too far from the entrance. As we moved closer, I caught sight of an array of hats, necklaces, watches, and other adornments—yet, alas, no bows so far. I felt a flutter of disappointment, but I pushed it down, determined to keep searching.

My mom had wandered off to the women's section on the next aisle, likely looking for pieces that might catch her eye. Meanwhile, I took it upon myself to hunt through the accessories in search of the perfect bows. Now, you might be thinking the odds of stumbling upon a glow-in-the-dark bow at a brick-and-mortar store were almost nonexistent, and you'd be absolutely right. It felt like looking for a needle in a haystack, but that did not deter me. Our plan was to purchase the bows plain and then invite Jay and Liyah over to my house for a crafting party, where we could attach glow sticks around them together. With determination in my heart, I continued scanning the shelves.

"Excuse me, do you guys have any bows?" I kindly ask a worker.

"Umm, yes we do right around here." He points me around the corner.

"Okay, thank you."

They had every color, shape and size of bows you could possibly imagine, even three shades of Orange! I didn't even know Orange had more than one shade. I found the light pink section and just on time my phone ringed.

"Hey Liyah!"

"Hey Arri!"

"So I'm out shopping, and I found like 6 different shades of pink we could choose from for the bows.

"Okay."

Jay still hadn't answered the call, so I just showed Liyah all the colors.

"Ou, that one right there, it looks just like the one Jay and I got." she says

"Looks like what Jay and you got?" I questioned.

"Oh yeah, she's over at my house right now, we're adding glow sticks to them." Liyah says, flipping her screen around to give me a glimpse of Jay carefully attaching the colorful glow sticks to the top of her bow.

"Oh, I thought we were going to go to my house and do it all together,"

"Yeah, but you know how Jay already lives right down the street from me, Plus, we got our bows a few days ago, so it just kind of worked out! It's fineee. No big deal! We're still all going to match and wear them together for the celebration anyways. Win-win, right?"

"Yeah, I suppose," I responded, my heart a little heavy.

I was a bit confused Had I missed something in our earlier conversations? Had they casually decided this while I was off in my own little world? I would've happily joined them if I had known that was the plan; after all, the fun of crafting these bows was all about sharing the experience.

But Liyah was right. Jay lived only about ten minutes from her, so it made practical sense for them to meet up and work on the bows together without a lengthy trek across town. Finishing the bows at her house was definitely more convenient… right?

Accepting the circumstances, I took a deep breath, trying to push away the feelings of exclusion and just focus on the fact that we would all eventually wear the same glowing bows together. I'd just have to pick up my bow, jazz it up my own way, and then head home. It wasn't the group spectacle I had envisioned, but the celebration awaited us, and that was what truly mattered. My focus shifted to what I could do next and how I could make my bow stand out, even if I had to work on it solo.

The following week of school was the week of the celebration, it was on Friday. and then the Monday after was graduation. My mom took my sister and I over to my grandparents' house to see them since my great grandma wouldn't be able to make it to my graduation. She was more on the older side and had to use a walker but it was okay because I liked going over to their house anyways. The pool is humongous.

"Hey my little grandbabies!" my moms dad cheerfully announced. That was his name for us, his "little grandbabies". I mean I thought it was kind of cute, but my sister Monney always thought it was kind of silly.

"Hi papa!" we say in unison to him.

"So are my girls ready to go swimming or what? Grandma's cutting up some watermelon right now in the kitchen for you guys. Go change into your bathing suit upstairs and meet us in the backyard."

"Okay papa."

Okay, wait, to help with any confusion, my mom dad and his wife used to live alone together up by the mountains but when my grandma's dad got sick and passed, they moved with my great grandma by the far side to help take care of her and keep her company. Which was overall better for my grandma and us. It was a shorter drive plus my mom said growing up there used to be a few mountain lions up by them. And me and wild animals do not mix well.

Monney and I started to head upstairs to put on our bathing suits. My grandparents' house was beautiful. The carpet upstairs was nice and soft, giving your feet a break from the hard, wood floors downstairs. The bathrooms always had a nice smelling candle ready to be lit with pretty teal towels hanging on the rack. I loved my grandparents' house. The only downside was the amount of shedding the dogs did, I mean I could understand if it was every once and a while but it was like every time I sat down on the couch some fur was attached to my clothes ready to go home with me. My mom said it was because we mainly visited during the summertime and they were shedding their winter coats but still, I didn't wanna leave with a whole new outfit. My grandparents had three dogs. Izzy, Skittles and Chewy. I could never remember who was the oldest out of Skittles and Izzy but I was 99.9% sure it was Izzy. He was more grumpy and lazy one but secretly had the biggest heart ever. Chewy was the baby. Always so ready to play and jump around everywhere. Sometimes it got annoying but once you knew that he was just excited and a baby, it was easier to understand.

"Last one in the pool is a rotten egg! Monney screams at me as she starts running down the stairs.

"Well, it won't be me!" I scream as I slide down the railing.

The smell of freshly cut watermelon hit our noses the second that we set foot outside.

"Hi girls! Watermelon, strawberries and pineapples are all on the table by the patio." my grandma joyfully announces.

The whole day was filled with laughter, fruit, and a splash of color. The sun filtered through the trees, casting playful shadows on the ground as my grandpa worked his magic in the kitchen, happily cooking up dinner. The delicious aromas wafting from the stove made everyone's stomachs rumble in anticipation. Meanwhile, my mom was catching up with my aunt and uncle, sharing stories and reliving old memories. Time slipped by until my great-grandma finally made her way downstairs after spending the majority of the day in bed. We didn't take it personally; we understood that every time she lifted a finger, it took every ounce of strength she had—both mentally and physically.

"Hi, my lovelies," my great-grandma greeted us with a gentle smile that radiated warmth.

"Hi, Grandma! How are you feeling today?" We all chimed in unison, the way we had done since we were little, hoping to woo a smile and a story from her. She always told the best stories, I remember one time I was so deep into her story; I felt like it was me living it.

"I'm feeling good," she said, her voice soft yet strong. "Happy to see my family all in one place enjoying each other's company."

We all smiled back at her, our hearts full as we fixed our plates and gathered around the table. My papa had prepared his famous asparagus, perfectly grilled steak, and fluffy rice. Oh boy, did he love his asparagus. There was always a larger than necessary serving on his plate, as if it were the crown jewel of his culinary endeavors. As we ate, we took turns sharing updates on one another's lives—our work, new interests, and friends.

But as the topic shifted to friendships, I felt myself growing a little quiet. I hadn't really known what to say. Earlier that day, I had called Liyah and Jay. I wanted to show them the diving board, but they didn't answer. I felt worried until I saw them post a video together just minutes after my call—my heart sank as I watched them splashing around in Jays pool together, laughter echoing through the screen. I hadn't received an invite, which stung more than I cared to admit. Surely, it hadn't been intentional; they probably assumed I would be busy this weekend, and, to be fair, they weren't entirely wrong. So, I pushed the nagging thoughts aside for the time being and tried to focus on my family around me.

After dinner, as everyone buzzed with post-meal chatter, my great-grandma turned to me with a gentle look. "Will you help me with the cleanup, dear?" she asked. Her eyes were tired but filled with gratitude, and I couldn't say no.

"Of course, Grandma. I'd love to help," I replied, getting up from the table and following her into the kitchen.

"Thank you for helping me tidy up, you know grandma's hips are bad."

"Of course grandma, I have no problem helping. I like wiping down the counters. It makes me feel like I'm in one of those cleaning commercials showing why Lysol was the best cleaning product."

"Oh my, I love your big imagination and I'm sure your friends do too huh?" she asks in a curious yet invading way. I knew she had to notice how quiet I got when friends were bought up at the dinner table.

"Yeah.. I'm sure they do." I responded hesitating to look at her.

"Hey I know you're growing up and you might not want to communicate everything with me or even your parents for that matter but just always remember we're always going to be here. Right by your side through the good and the bad. Friends are always good to have but make sure they're as good to you as you are them.. Okay lovely?"

"Okay grandma."

We finished cleaning up and said our goodbyes to the family, parting our separate ways. I couldn't stop thinking about my grandma and what she told me during the ride home. I mean I'm sure Liyah and Jay treated me as I treated them. We were best friends. I think? Yes, I'm sure. Times must've been different for grandma. Friends back then probably weren't as nice and didn't share their triple-double stuffed pudding cup with each other but my friends did. My friends loved me and I loved my friends.

The next day at school was pretty chill. We watched a video on how to open lockers and know where our classes are for next year. Preparing more and more everyday to be in middle school.

"Hi Arri!" Lila and Jas say as they walk up to me in class. I had come to school a little late, my mom had accidently forgotten to set the alarm the night before so I didn't get to see them in the morning.

"Hey guys, how was swimming yesterday?" I asked them.

"Oh it was fun, sorry we didn't invite you it was just so last minute. We didn't even know we were going to swim." says Lila

"Oh that's okay, I'm just glad that you guys had fun!"

"Sooo, are we all ready for celebration? Everyone got their bows and glow sticks?" proclaims Lila.

"Yes, I made mine last night after I got back from my grandma's house. Pink with the white glow stick right?" I asked

"Yes, perfect!" Jas says.

We were all ready and prepared to have the best school day of our 5th grade lives.. Well besides our graduation of course. And next thing we knew… It was the day of the celebration…

Chapter 3

Celebration Day

We all met up for breakfast that morning before school, eager to load up on a good meal before diving into a day filled with popcorn and candy. It required waking up a little earlier than usual, but none of us minded. I slipped on my black leggings and a bright pink top.

After breakfast, my mom kindly gave us all a ride to school. "Okay, bye girls! I hope you all have a great day and have fun at the celebration!" my mom said cheerfully as she dropped us off.

"Okay, thank you! Bye!" We all said

As we headed towards the entrance, Jay broke the chatter, her brows furrowing in a mock-serious expression. "Do you guys actually think we're going to do work today?"

"I hope not!" I replied, sharing in her playful disbelief. The thought of sitting through a regular day of classes felt almost ludicrous when the celebration loomed so close.

"I mean, it's the day of the celebration, they'd have to be crazy to make us do any real work. Right?" Agreed Liyah.

"Right!" We all agreed.

Realistically, I knew it wasn't likely we could have a full day of partying, but I clung to the hope that maybe our teachers would let us watch some videos or do some fun activities to get us into the celebratory spirit, at least until the afternoon. Who knows? Perhaps they'd line up CSN10 videos or organize some school-themed games before we finally headed off to the main event. The possibilities of a fun school day kept our energy high as we bounced through the halls, anticipation building with each step we took toward our classrooms.

"Good morning, ladies and gents!" Mrs. G says welcoming us into the classroom.

"Who's all excited for today's celebration??"

"ME! ME! ME!", everyone in the classroom screamed. We all have been waiting for this day for the past month and finally it was here.

"Okay so I know a lot of you guys are confused about today's agenda until the party so I'm going to tell you. Yes, we are still going to do some form of learning today—

"NOOOOO" the class all lets out as a collective. None of us wanted to do that.

"Come on Mrs. G" Allen says.

"I'm sorry but this is still an official school day, what do I always say?"

"Work now and have fun later." the class utters in dismay.

"Yes, exactly! Don't worry, us teachers aren't completely evil, it's not like a test or anything. Everyone open your Chromebook and click the link in google classroom.'

I wasn't complaining too much about having to do school work. My dad used to say the same thing, how if you do your work now then you can have fun later. I never really understood it when I was younger but now it made sense. It feels more rewarding that way anyways.

I clicked the link in the classroom and was brought to a wonderful surprise... KAHOOT! Oh every kid loved kahoot. I think even high schoolers even did too. It was this game where the teachers would put a question up on the screen and you had four different choices to choose from.

Example: What number comes after 9, Red= 7, Orange= 10, Yellow=5, Blue=1.(You would obviously click yellow).

First you joined the game through the class code and waited in the waiting room until everyone joined. Points were also based on whoever answered correctly first. So the faster you answered the questions correctly the more points you would get and you would stay on the podium. There's also a time limit though. You get 25 seconds to answer the question, so the pressure was definitely on. Then at the end of the game, the top 3 players on the podium got jolly ranchers (this was completely dependent on your teacher though). Mrs. G always made sure we got some candy after we won. It was the best form of learning honestly in my opinion.

"Okay here's the class code to join the game.

"QHU890" The code read out on the whiteboard. I always had a personal race with the other kids to be first in the lobby, just because I like seeing my name pop up first.

I hurriedly typed in the code on my Chromebook, feeling the rush of competition surge through me. My heart raced as I hit "Join," and I was in with a triumphant smile plastered across my face as I saw my name flash on the screen. !

"Don't get too cocky now, Arri! I'm coming for you!" Jay chimed from her seat, a confident grin plastered on her face.

"Oh, we'll see about that!" I replied, narrowing my eyes in mock seriousness, trying to hold back laughter.

Look who's always the first one in!" Liyah giggled as she joined in after me. "You're so competitive, Arri."

"Hey, someone has to take home the candy!" I replied playfully.

Mrs. G clicked the button to start the game, revealing the first question. It was a breeze—basic multiplication, something we had mastered weeks ago. I quickly tapped the correct answer and thundered ahead in points.

"Ha, look who's in first place Jay... Meee!" I taunt Jay.

"Yeah yeah, whatever. Save it for the next question."

Which is the value of 7 x 6?" Mrs. G announced with a grin as the answers appeared.

"42! It's 42!" I blurted out, eager to get my answer in first. I whipped my finger over the option and held my breath as the timer counted down, hoping I got it right.

"OH YEAHHH, LETSSS GOO!" I chant. Who's not winning?? Not me!! Oh yeah, Oh yeah, Oh yeah...

So... completely ignore my last initial statement. I'm not sure if Jay could see the future and no one knew, but as the rounds continued, the questions started getting trickier and trickier. We moved from multiplication to fractions, then spiraled into word problems that needed more calculation than I anticipated. Next thing I know, I'm running out of time to answer the questions because I'm stuck on dumb PEMDAS. (For everyone who didn't have a traumatizing math experience, PEDMAS was these steps we had to follow to solve a multi-step equation. It was Parentheses, Exponents, Division, Multiplication, Addition, and Subtraction, in that order.) After a few math questions the horror was finally over and we transitioned to an English grammar game.

"Okay, time to brush up on our parts of speech!" Mrs. G said with excitement, and we couldn't help but chuckle at our not-so-sneaky transition from math to grammar. Mrs. G loved English, just like me.

"Come on, Arri! You can do it!" Liyah cheered, squinting at her screen as she too battled for the top spot.

Through the highs and lows of the game, we laughed together and found that the friendly rivalry fueled us. Though my score started to slide, the fun was evident and it wasn't about winning. I remarked out loud, "It was the excitement of being involved, of playing together as a class," but let's just say it was different in my brain ha-ha.

Once we finished Kahoot, we shifted gears to another game focusing on English grammar. This time, it was a team-based challenge, so I was relieved to switch from individual pressure to group collaboration.

"I'll take charge with verb tenses!" I asserted as the game began.

"I'm on nouns!" Liyah replied, and Jay grinned as she chimed in, "And I'll be our resident punctuation expert."

Together, we tackled the questions, piecing together phrases and correcting errors. There were cheers of triumph when we answered correctly and playful banter when we made mistakes.

After the games, Mrs. G beckoned us back to our seats, her smile radiating warmth.

"Now, to cap off the fun, we're going to dive into our final reading of 'Charlotte's Web'! I want everyone to really pay attention to the story, so we can wrap up our time with Wilbur and Fern properly."

We've been reading Charlotte's Web for months and finally we're going to know the end. It was kind of bittersweet. I was eager to know the end of course. If Wilbur's life would be saved or not, or even what would happen to Charlotte. The suspense got me every time, but after I found out then what? It would be an ending to an adventure that I didn't know if I was prepared for or not.

As the last pages turned, and Charlotte took her final farewell, I felt that familiar lump in my throat rising. I blinked rapidly, trying to stave off the tears that threatened to spill.

"Why do all the best stories make us feel like this?" I whispered, my voice cracking.

"I know, right? I can't believe she has to go," Liyah replied, her eyes mirroring my sorrow.

And then it happened. As the final lines closed, the room filled with muffled sniffs and sorrowful sighs. It was as if the collective weight of our emotions pressed us all together in that chair. I could feel the sting of tears well up, and I let one slip down my cheek.

"I always cry at the end—because it's just so beautiful and sad. But mostly, I don't want the story to end," I murmured to my friends.

"Me too, Arri!" Jay replied, her expression softened by empathy.

Mrs. G stood up with a warm smile, her voice steady but filled with emotion as she addressed the class.

"Alright, everyone, settle down for a moment! I know that finishing Charlotte's Web has left us all feeling a bit heavy-hearted. It's perfectly natural to feel sad when something we love comes to an end. I want you to take a moment to reflect on what we've experienced together through this story. Wilbur, Charlotte, and all of their friends have taught us so much about friendship, loyalty, and even the bittersweet nature of life. As we feel these emotions, remember that endings are not purely a thing of sorrow. They are, in fact, a vital part of the journey. Just like the changing seasons, where autumn gives way to the vibrancy of winter and the promise of spring, endings often make space for new beginnings. Charlotte's wonderful legacy does not end with her passing; it continues through Wilbur and the many lives he will touch. Now, let's make some joyful memories together and celebrate not just what we've finished, but what lies ahead for all of us!"

Eventually, the moment passed, and Mrs. G announced, "Alright, everyone! It's time to celebrate!"

I think that was Mrs. G way of telling us how much she'll miss us after graduation. It was almost like she was trying to remind herself that change is a part of life and it's okay to be sad about it but also see the positive. Either way, it was nice and kind. It really brightened up the energy and made everyone feel a little better about the book.

The classroom soon buzzed with energy as we eagerly prepared for the party. "Oh my gosh, I can't wait!" I said.

Our teachers were so understanding. They made sure even those who lost their privileges still got to partake in all the fun. They reminded us that "Everyone deserves a second chance."

We helped Mrs. G set up the final things for her classroom. It was pretty much already set up, we just needed to rearrange all the bean bags and put them in the middle of the classroom. The desks were already separated and out of the way for the most part, besides the few that some students decided to sit in during kahoot. Every teacher had snacks in their room already set out and yes mom, I made sure to read every ingredient before I even thought about opening it. No allergy attack on my watch.

Before we began, all of our teachers explained the rules and regulations of the party.

"1- Don't be too loud. Other classes in this school are still learning and going on, we must respect them as we would want them to respect us.

2- This isn't free for all. We are still in school so we will still be following all the rules and regulations of the school. Act with respect and some common sense.

3- Make sure to clean up after ourselves. All trash should be ending up in the trashcan where it belongs.

4- Have fun! Enjoy your last Friday of the fifth grade. You guys deserve it. Now go on and enjoy your time!

"Well, where do you guys want to go first? Ask Liyah.

"Do you guys want to start off with the board game room?" Jay said

"Yes, I think then after that we could go to the party room and the movie room last so we can do all the activities."

"Okay yes I agree." the rest of the group announced.

The game room was set up as Candyland. Mrs. V had added pink and blue rugs by the entrance of the door. She had also had a station where we could make candy necklaces.

"What game do you guys want to play first? Uno, Goldfish or Spades?" Jay questioned

The card games were the first things by the entrances so we decided to go with that category.

"Mhmm, Uno doesn't sound too bad," exclaims Liyah.

"Alright, so Uno it is!" Liyah said, a spark of excitement in her eyes. "I'll shuffle the cards!"

We gathered around a small table, the colorful and inviting atmosphere of the Candyland-themed room buzzing with energy. The pink and blue rugs made the space feel whimsical, almost like stepping into a storybook. I looked around at the decorations - oversized candy canes and rainbow streamers hung from the ceiling, all contributing to the sweet vibe.

"Ugh, I can't believe Mrs. V went all out with this," I said, smiling. "This is amazing!"

As Liyah shuffled, Jay eyed the candy necklace station. "We should definitely make those before we leave here. Candy jewelry??? Yeahhh, those will be going home with me tonight."

"Exactly!" I replied, nodding vigorously. "Plus, they'll be a great party snack for later."

"Okay, okay, I promise we'll get to the candy necklaces next," Liyah said, placing the shuffled Uno cards down. "But first, let's see who is the true Uno champion!"

As we played, the laughter and playful banter filled the room. Each time someone drew a "Draw Four" card, the dramatic gasps were met with a volley of good-natured mock outrage.

"NO WAY!" Jay exclaimed dramatically when Liyah played the card on her. "That's it! I'm coming for you next round!"

"Bring it on!" Liyah shot back, grinning widely.

After a few rounds, we declared Jay the champion. "Alright, Uno is fun, but we must make those candy necklaces!" Jay insisted, dragging us toward the sparkling table filled with colorful treats.

We rushed over, and I excitedly grabbed the Airhead rainbow candies. The best candy known to mankind!

"This is going to taste incredible," Liyah said, already working on her own masterpiece, filled with gummy bears and sour strings.

"Save some for me, Arri!" Jay said, giving me puppy eyes as she worked on her own necklace.

Once we each completed our candy creations, the activity seemed to wrap up just in time for Mrs. G to remind us of the time

"Alright everyone! You're welcomed to stay in the room where you're at already if you would like but Mrs. H room is now set up for anyone who would like to read or nap."

"Um, who was going to nap during this amazing celebration?" I asked

"Right, especially with all this CANDYYY!" exclaimed Jay.

"Uh Jay… maybe you should've not made a candy necklace actually…" Liyah and I say in unison.

"Yeah, yeah, yeah, anyway where to next?"

"Do you guys want to head to the party room?" Liyah suggested.

"Definitely! Let's dance it out!" said Jay, already feeling the rhythm of the music echoing from the next room.

"Onward, to the party room!" Jay proclaimed dramatically.

As we entered the party room, the atmosphere shifted instantly. Bright balloons danced from the ceiling, and a colorful banner reading "CELEBRATE OUR ADVENTURES AND NEW BEGINNING!" hung proudly across one wall. A disco ball spun overhead, casting playful beams of light that twinkled like stars.

Liyah squealed in delight. "Look at all the decorations! It feels like a real party in here! Even though the closest thing I've been to that was like a party was my cousin's quince Nera but still."

The beat of the music pulsed through the air, inviting us to the center of the room, where a dance floor awaited. "Come on! Let's dance!" I beckoned. The melody was infectious, and soon we were all moving to the rhythm, arms thrown in the air and laughter spilling out like confetti.

"Okay, okay, but someone teach me these dance moves!" Jay shouted over the music, pretending to struggle. "I need a lesson!"

"What are you doing?" I laughed, mimicking her awkward shuffling as Liyah cheered and clapped her hands.

"The only dances I know are the ones I watch on Musically, and even then I mess up at least 50 times before I post it." laughs Jay.

"Just dance like no one's watching!" Liyah chimed in, and we all burst into fits of laughter, letting the music wash over us.

After a few songs, Mrs. H stepped up to the front, her arms raised to quiet the room. "Alright, everyone! I hope you're having fun! After some dancing, we're going to have cake and snacks!"

"Cake?" We all cheered, our voices blending together

Mrs. H smiled, clearly delighted by our excitement.

"Yes, cake! And before we enjoy it, I want each of you to share your favorite part of today. It can be about the story, the games, or even this dance party! Who wants to start?"

"My favorite part of the day definitely has to be right now, aka the cake." A kid in my class named Brandon announced as we all chuckled at him.

"My favorite part was building candy necklaces with my friends, and being on a sugar rush," said Jay.

"Yeah, so maybe we should calm down on the sweets now, shouldn't we jay. Mrs. H and G laughed.

"Aha, well my favorite part was definitely when we read about Charlotte's farewell. It was so bittersweet, but then I got to see how we all felt so connected by it and that was pretty cool." I said.

Liyah chimed in next, "I also loved making the candy necklaces! It reminded me of how we used to make friendship bracelets when we were younger. Sharing the moment with you guys was the best part!"

"Dancing together is definitely my favorite!" Austin added, "This whole day has been a blast!"

One by one, we shared our thoughts, filling the room with warmth and reflections from our shared experience. And just as the last words were spoken, Mrs. G waved her hands again. "Alright, now that everyone has shared, it's time for the cake! Who's ready?"

Cheers erupted once more, and we rushed to the snack table, our hearts light as we grabbed plates. The sight of the chocolate and vanilla layered cake, adorned with bright frosting and sprinkled with stars, made our mouths water. Even though I hated chocolate cake, I didn't even mind. I finished all my cake.

As we gathered around, I caught a moment to glance at my friends, their faces lit with smiles—the sweet tip of the day's iceberg. From the tearful reading of Charlotte's Web to the thrilling dance party, we had created a beautiful memory.

With each bite of cake, I savored the taste of friendship, laughter, and the hopeful anticipation of all the new adventures that were yet to come. After all, as the story taught us, every ending truly is just a new beginning waiting to unfold.

Chapter 4

Graduation

The next two days were crucial. We only had Saturday, Sunday and then Monday was the day of graduation. I was spending the weekend at my dad's house, and there was just something special about weekends with him. I knew this one would be extra special—my graduation was just around the corner.

"Rise and shine, sleepyhead!" Dad called as he popped his head into my room. "We've got lots planned today, starting with a little pampering for you."

"Pampering?" I replied, rubbing the sleep from my eyes. "What do you mean?"

"I made an appointment for you to get your hair done. You mentioned wanting to straighten it, remember?" He prompted, giving me a smile that could brighten up the darkest day.

"Oh my gosh, yes! I'm so excited!" I jumped out of bed and quickly got ready. The thought of straightening my hair was unreal. Just as my excitement began bubbling over, I faced a slight hiccup in the plan. What will be the cutest top to take pictures in after I get my hair done? I couldn't wear just one of my plain white shirts, I had to wear something that gave "New Hair, New me."

Picking out the perfect cute top from my closet felt like choosing an outfit for the first day of school… and now that

I think about it, I'll be dealing with that headache in a few months.

"I can't decide which one looks the cutest!" I exclaimed, holding up two sparkly options.

"Just wear what makes you feel "fabulous," my dad chuckled, rolling his eyes at my mini fashion crisis.

"But they both make me feel fabulous, they're my best tops."

"Enny, Meany. Minny, Mo it." said my Monney.

"Monney, you know you're the smartest sister I've ever had?" I exclaimed.

"I'm the only sister you've ever had." she replied, rolling her eyes and continuing getting ready.

"Enny, Meany, Minny, Mo. Catch a tiger by his toe. If he hollers, let him go. Enny, Meany, Minny, Mo.

My black shirt with pink glittery hearts it was. I do love a good black shirt, so I was satisfied with my choice.

"Okay, are you guys ready? My stepmom asked.

"Yes, as ready as I'll ever be." I said.

We ambled over to the salon, and when we walked in, The vibes were already immaculate. I was greeted by an inviting, bright atmosphere. The place smelled of hair products and fresh muffins.

"Hey there! You must be Arrionna!" said the receptionist with a welcoming smile.

"Yep, that's me!" I chirped.

"Okay, perfect! Your stylist will be out soon, but in the meantime would any of you like one of our complimentary muffins?"

"MUFFINS?" My sister and I echoed together.

"We would love some!"

"Aha okay. We have Blueberry, Banana, Or Cinnamon,"

"Umm may I please have Banana?"

"And can I have Blueberry please?" Monney said

"Yes of course, I'll bring them out shortly.

"Your stylist will be out shortly. You're in for a treat!" she said, her eyes sparkling with enthusiasm

Stepping into the salon was like entering a magical realm of hair products, glossy magazine covers, and the sounds of hair dryers buzzing all around. The sweet but bitter smell of heat protectant ran through my nose.

"Hi, you must be excited! My name is Stacy and I'm your stylist for today. Let's get started!"

"Yes! So excited for my first straightening!" I replied

"So are you just getting your hair flat ironed for fun or is there a special occasion? Miss Stacy asked.

"Yes, my graduation is on Monday!"

"Oh my!! Congratulations!! Don't worry, we're going to get you right and ready for your graduation.

Later that afternoon, after what felt like an eternity, I finally emerged from the salon with my hair sleek and straight. I swung my hair back and forth, admiring the mirror's reflection.

"Whoa, look at that shine!" Dad exclaimed, grinning wide. "You look beautiful my love!"

"Thanks! My ends look a little shorter than I wanted, but I heard trimming is good for healthy hair…" I said, trying to hide my disappointment. Which was true, since it was my first ever hair appointment and first ever hair cut, I wasn't surprised by the need to let go of some dead ends.

"Absolutely! A little cut goes a long way in maintaining health. Just think of it as your hair's spring cleaning," he reassured me.

"You're right, I guess…" I sighed. We thanked Miss Stacey and the receptionist and got into the car. I couldn't stop running my fingers through my hair. It felt so nice and soft.

"Okay, where to next?" I asked my dad

"Well, I have good news and bad news, which one do you want first?"

"Uh oh… uh."

"Say bad news so you can end off a good note." my sister and stepbrother said."

"Oh, you're right, okay I'll take the bad news first."

"Okay well the bad news is your cousins won't be able to make it to your graduation, they're starting their summer vacations a little earlier, so they won't be in town."

"Okay… so I'm starting to regret hearing any news at all now." I said, with my face beginning to scrunch up.

"Well, that sucks because I was just going to tell you that the good news is we are going over to their house right now so you could see them before your graduation at least but you know we could just go home…"

"YAYYYY NO I WAS JUST KIDDING! I LOVE NEWS!." I replied, my face lightening back up.

"Well are you sure because—"

"I'm a 1000% positive dad.

"Aha, thought so. Okay well let's be on our way."

When we arrived at my cousins' house, they were already waiting for us outside by the garage.

"ARRI AND MONNEY!" they yelled, running up to us and hugging us tightly.

"NIYA AND NEVAEH!" my sister and I replied, the excitement bubbling over like soda pop.

"OMG, you got your hair done? It looks amazing!" Niya squealed, squeezing me in a hug that practically lifted me off the ground.

"Thank you!" I beamed, feeling like a star.

"I just know you're going to look so cute at your graduation…" Neveah added, her eyes sparkling with excitement.

"We can't believe you're growing up and leaving fifth grade! What are you going to do now?" Niya asked, her curiosity bubbling over.

"Oh, I've been asked that non-stop! Honestly, I have no idea how I feel about it," I admitted, glancing at Monney for support. "I guess I'm excited and a little scared too."

"Same! But no worries, we're all going through it together!" Niya reassured me, her contagious confidence pushing away my lingering doubts.

She was one grade below me, so her time to graduate was coming up soon too. The question "Are you ready to graduate?" felt like an indirect challenge that I could never quite figure out how to answer.

"Well, what do you guys want to do?" Monney asked, breaking the sentimental mood.

"I know I'm kind of hungry; do you guys still have those spicy chicken tenders with fries your mom made us last time?" I asked, my stomach growling at the memory.

"Uhhh, duh! Let's make some!" Niya declared, leading the way into the kitchen.

We rushed inside and began rummaging through the pantry and fridge, pulling out ingredients like we were on some sort of culinary treasure hunt. The spicy chicken tenders were golden on the outside and had a satisfying crunch that hinted at their zesty flavor, while the fries were thick-cut and crispy, coated in salt that practically twinkled under the kitchen light. These were not just any plain chicken fingers and fries, these were life.

Okay, so I'm actually not the best cook out of the bunch, so they put me on the plating duty. Yes I know... I'm the oldest... but listen... cooking was hard.

"Don't worry, Arri! I've seen you plate things before; it's a vital skill!" Neveah teased. I rolled my eyes but chuckled along, knowing they were right. Maybe one day I'd be whipping up meals like a top chef, but for now, I'd keep it simple.

While the chicken tended to its frying destiny, we decided to have some fun. We cranked up the music and started filming mini dance videos in the kitchen, grooving to the rhythm as we pretended, we were in a big music video.

"Niya, do that spin again!" I laughed as she twirled and tossed her hair dramatically.

"I'm gonna have the best moves for our music video!" Niya said, cutting a few playful moves that we couldn't stop laughing at.

Beep Beep

"Food's ready!" Money shouted from the kitchen.

After a glorious multi-course meal, filled with spicy chicken tenders and crispy fries, we sprawled on the couch, feeling full and content.

"Alright, who's up for a scary movie?" Neveah suggested, her eyes glinting with mischief.

"Let's do it!" I replied, eager. The thrill of a scary movie felt like the perfect cap to our day.

"Nope, no way. You guys know I hate scary movies." Monney said in disgust

"Me too." Niya agreed

"Come on guys, it'll be fun and it's not even that dark outside so there is nothing to be afraid of."

"Ugh. Okay fine but if it gets too scary then I'm turning it off." They both agreed.

"YAY, okay fair!" Neveah and I said.

We picked the movie "The Boy". It was like a different version of Chucky or Annabelle but more suspenseful with a lot of jump scares. So, we quickly found ourselves all bunched up together clutching each other's arms as eerie music filled the room. It was probably not the best idea to choose a horror film after a big meal, considering how quickly our stomachs started bubbling but the excitement of it all definitely made it worth it.

"Why do they always investigate the creepy noise?" I whispered, my heart racing as I faced the screen.

"Because they're all super dumb! Just run!" Monney exclaimed, and we all giggled at the absurdity of the characters' choices.

"Yeah, if that ever happens to me, I'm running away the first chance I get." laughed Neveah

"Well, I hope that never happens to us. "says Niya nervously laughing.

Once the credits rolled and the lights flickered back on, we all agreed that we needed to shake off the eerie vibes.

"Let's go jump on the trampoline." Monney suggests.

"Jumping on the trampoline sounds perfect to me!" I declared, eager to escape the frightful atmosphere.

Outside, the moon hung high in the sky, and it felt like we were in our own little world on the trampoline.

"Let's play crack the egg." said Nevaeh

"No, that game always hurts my head." complained Niya.

"Ok then let's play truth or dare jumping style."

"Okay, I dare you, Niya!" I announced, adrenaline pumping through my veins. "You have to jump from the trampoline into the pool!"

Niya's eyes sparkled with her usual daring energy. "You're on!" she said confidently, taking a few hops before leaping from the trampoline. We all gasped as she landed with a spectacular splash that sent water spraying everywhere. Niya was always the adventurous type out of us. If we told her to go run up to a random stranger in the store and talk in a British voice asking them where the toilet paper is, she would do it without a doubt.

"Whoa! You actually did it!" Monney exclaimed, clapping her hands in amazement as we hurried to the pool's edge to ensure she was okay.

"Duh, of course I did. Now get me a towel because our parents come downstairs and see the mess, we made aha!" Niya yelled, swimming back to the ladder, and we raced to find one, running back inside the house to grab it quickly before we got caught.

After Niya dried off, headed up for a shower.

My uncle had an arcade room so we went in there while Niya showered, trying to pass the time.

The arcade room was a haven of bright lights and pulsing sounds, and we dove right into a game of air hockey. The adrenaline from earlier still buzzed in our veins as we tried to outscore each other.

After a few intense rounds, time passed away from us quicker than we expected.

"Come on girls! Time to head back home." My dad yelled from downstairs.

"Aww, we have to go now." I said sadly

"It's okay, we'll see each other soon and have a lot of sleepovers during the summer. I'll tell Niya that you guys are leaving. I love you guys so much and congratulations Arri. I know you're going to do great and big things." my cousin sweetly announced.

"We love you more." Monney and I said in unison.

We made our way downstairs, reluctantly preparing to leave our exciting day behind.

"I had the best time, guys! We need to do this more often," I said, feeling grateful for the fun-filled day spent with my favorite cousins.

As we piled into the car, I glanced back, waving goodbye to Niya and Neveah. With all the laughter, adventures, and a few heart-pounding moments from the day, I felt a warmth in my heart, and it was clear that spending time with family always made everything better.

"Did you guys have fun with your cousins?' my dad asked.

"Yesss it was so much fun, Niya even jumped in the pool.' I exclaimed

"Oh my, you guys didn't get water everywhere right?" he asked, laughing.

"Noo, we brought her out a towel." Monney exclaimed.

"I wish we did stuff like that, all we did was play video games and feed the snakes." my step brother said.

"Well, I've always been afraid of snakes so you're braver than me, " I said.

We all laughed and continued the journey back home.

"Make sure to get some good sleep!" my dad called out, "We have a big day tomorrow."

◆

The next morning, Sunday arrived with the same eventful energy.

"Alright, sleepyheads! We're going shopping for your graduation outfit!" my dad announced, a wide grin stretching across his face.

I practically jumped out of my seat. "Yay! Can we go to the Fashion Show Mall?"

"Of course! Wherever you need to go to find the perfect outfit."

Yay. I was so excited I almost forgot to put on socks with my sneakers.

Once we got to the mall, the first thing I spotted was Wetzel's Pretzels.

"Dad, I need a pretzel first!"

"Go for it, kiddo. Just don't fill up too much!" Dad chuckled, watching as I devoured my snack. I loved their slushies and cinnamon pretzels; it was like eating a cloud full of heaven.

After I finished up my snack we headed towards the upstairs of the mall.

"Hey dad, where are we going?" I asked, looking at all the dress shops we were passing.

"We're going to a store." my dad said facetiously

My dad was big on surprises, and I had come to realize that accepting them was part of our unique father-daughter bond. There was a certain thrill in not knowing what to expect, especially when it came to special occasions. Today was one of those days—I could feel the excitement building inside me as I waited to discover the surprise he had in store.

After five minutes or so we finally stopped in front of a store.

"Customizable T- shirts" I read on a sign inside of it.

"So, would you prefer a white or black shirt for your outfit?" Dad asked.

"Um, wait. Aren't we looking for a dress?" I replied, confused…. "A pink dress at that, " I say in my head.

"You'll see! Just pick a color," he insisted.

"Okay. Black, then?" I decided, still puzzled but willing to go along with my dad's plan.

"Okay perfect." the worker announced.

First things first, what's your favorite color?

"Uh, red." I say in a snarky way. Part of me was kind of upset that I was just getting a shirt for my graduation day. I envisioned a big nice outfit, and this was the opposite.

'Okay and do you like glitter or gold?"

"I mean gold is pretty nice."

"Perfect."

The worker then began typing on his computer really fast. The sounds of clicks and keyboard typing started to fill the room.

"And spell your name for me please." he said

"A-r-r-i-o-n-n-a."

"Okay, thank you."

After a few moments or so the worker turned his computer towards me and started to showcase the cool designs and ideas he had created. I felt my curiosity spark anew as I browsed. The possibilities seemed endless—gold, bright graphics, and even bold lettering.

I loved the idea of having my name emblazoned on the front in swirly letters, flanked by my favorite colors—red, of course!

"These are awesome." my dad said. "Now let's take some of these ideas and make it special," Dad said, his eyes twinkling as we chose the design. Together, we meticulously selected the colors and details, chatting excitedly about how the shirt would turn out. It felt so personal—like a blank canvas turning into a piece of art that was distinctly mine. The anticipation only grew as I envisioned what this shirt would represent: my journey, achievements, and all the milestones that had led to this moment. The idea transformed from mere fabric into a piece of my story.

"This is going to be awesome!" I thought, the earlier confusion fading away as excitement washed over me.

After we finally finished up the design of my shirt the worker told us it would be ready in about an hour or so, so we decided to head over to a different store to find some bottoms for my shirt.

"Where do you want to go?" my dad asked.

Since I wasn't wearing a dress, I still wanted to fit in with the "girly" look, so I wanted to wear a skirt. I had to find something that didn't give "old lady in a church" but also didn't give "just turned 21 and I'm heading to the club."

"Hmm, let's go to Forever 21." Forever 21 was a "teen" store. It was a mix between junior high and high school fashion trends all put together in one store and since I was going into one of those, I thought it only made sense to look in there.

"Okay, let's go." my father said.

I didn't know what color skirt I should get though. Black on black seemed a little too much and a regular jean skirt wouldn't look good paired with all the designs and shimmers in my shirt.

"Excuse me, can you help me find the "dressy" attire? I asked one of the workers nearby.

"Yeah of course!" she said.

She guided me over by fragrances and purses, to the left of them were the dresses, skirts and button ups.

"Thank you so much." I told her as she walked away

I browsed through all the items. They were color coded and racked by size. The problem was I didn't know what color I wanted, just that I wanted a skirt.

After what felt like years, I finally found what I was looking for. There it sat by the white button up blouses, a denim, white skirt. It looked perfect. It wasn't too long or two short. It sat right before my knees with a perfect aligned stitch.

"Dad! I found the most perfect skirt ever." I say to him as I run up to him.

"Woah that's a nice skirt, you're going to look so nice." my sister said.

"Aww, thank you Monney."

"Okay! Now let's go to the checkout. We still have a little bit of time until your shirt is ready so we can see some other stores and then head up to grab your shirt. But we have to hurry up so we can go to the next store and get you your shoes."

"Okay."

I really wanted some nice earrings to go with my outfits so we went to Claires. I loved Claries. They always have the best jewelry, well in my opinion. I remember my grandma bought me a butterfly necklace from them last year. It even glowed in the dark!... but the dogs got to it and I never saw it again.. So I definitely will be keeping my new earrings far away from them.

"Hi excuse me, do you guys have any white-like small earrings?" I asked the lady at the cash register.

"Yes! You're actually in luck because we just restocked last month on our white pieces."

"Yay, perfect thank you so much"

She pointed me to the corner where all the white jewelry was and in almost an instant, I found the perfect earrings.

Gold framed with white covered pearls. Absolutely beautiful.

Finally, it was time to pick up my customizable shirt.

When I saw how it turned out, my heart soared. "I love it!" I exclaimed. For a moment, I completely forgot about how I wanted to match with my friends.

"I knew we'd create something special together," Dad brought up, beaming with pride.

"And that we definitely did." I say smiling back at him.

The front of my shirt read "Ms. Queen Arrionna" in yellow letters with a red outline, dripping from the words. It was so beautiful. It was spray painted but only enough to where it still gave off its subtle and showy style. I couldn't take my eyes off of it.

"Anything that you guys wanna fix?" the worker asked

"No, not at all. Everything is perfect. I love it.

"Good! I'm glad."

After we had checked out we headed back downstairs towards the parking lot, which was kind of confusing but I didn't understand why we would go into a different mall to get shoes when there were a ton of shoe stores in this mall.

I didn't even know what shoes I wanted to wear. I know I wasn't going to wear sandals or wedges because that wouldn't go too well with my outfits but I didn't know what other options there were.

After being in the car for a while, we finally stopped in front of the new mall.

"The Forum Shops At Caesars". I remember going to this mall when I was younger but only when my dad went shopping for some new clothes or we wanted to watch the fire and water show.

"Where are we going dad?" I asked him

"Just enjoy the walk and follow me," he told me.

"Okay."

Even though I wanted to do the complete opposite of that, I listened.

"Okay, come on." my dad announced as he pulled me into the store.

"VERSACE" it read.

Woah. This was a grown-up store. This was the store where my dad would go and spend a lot of money. What were we doing here?

"Hello Cross!" called out a lady coming from the backroom.

"Hi Mimi!" my dad responded

"I see you brought your girls! Finally I get to meet them."

"Yes, I know, this is Arri and Monney."

"Hii." my sister and I say in unison.

"Soo which one of you guys are graduating?"

"Me." I replied.

"Okay, well perfect because your dad and I have a special gift made just for you."

Mimi went into the back of the store and came back out with a yellow box with a red bow on top.

"Here you go, this is for you."

I looked back at my dad, nodding his head in approval to open up the box. I grabbed the box and set it on the counter, making sure to carefully unravel the bow, not messing it up. The top of the box felt like silk but graphic at the same time. It was heavy yet light. I took the top off the box and removed the white tissue paper that covered the shoes. Yellow, black and white colors emerged from the box.

"Well, what do you think?" my dad asked me.

I pulled one shoe out of the box and glanced at each design. The shoe lances were white and strong. They weren't like any regular shoe laces I've ever had. The shoe felt heavy. A gold medusa chain sat at the ankle with black designs filling out the rest of the shoe.

"I'm speechless, I love them. They're so different but simple?"

"I'm glad, because they're going to be your graduation shoes."

"No way. REALLY, these shoes are so nice though. What if I get them dirty?"

"Well good thing they invited shoe cleaners, aha. But still be careful. These are nice shoes so take care of them like you value them."

"Of course I will dad. Thank you so much! I love you."

"I love you more, and don't worry honey, soon as you graduate, you'll be right here too.

"I'll rather just get a bunch of slime but yay okay." Monney responds.

We all laughed and finally started heading home. I couldn't wait to try on my entire outfit with my shoes. I called my mom as soon as I got in my room to show her.

"Oh my! You look stunning, honey!" She said over FaceTime. "That skirt is perfect for your graduation! I can't wait to see it in person!"

"Thank you, mommy! And look at my new shoes that dad got me."

"Oh those are nice, they match your shirt perfectly too."

"I know right! I just can't wait for my graduation tomorrow."

"Me either honey, make sure you get some good sleep tonight okay."

"Okay, goodnight mom, I love you."

"I love you more."

As the day wrapped up, my excitement flared again. I was ready for graduation.

"Tomorrow's the big day!" I announced to Dad, practically bouncing on my toes.

"It sure is! You're going to shine! I'm so proud of you," he said, as he gave me a kiss and hug goodnight. As I lay in bed that night, thinking about all the moments leading up to this day, I couldn't shake the excitement coursing through me. I was ready to take that leap; to walk across that stage and embrace the new beginnings waiting ahead.

Chapter 5

Bye-Bye Fifth Grade

The blaring alarm jolted me awake, penetrating the sleepy haze that clung to my mind. I glanced at the clock, and my heart skipped a beat when I saw the bright red numbers glowing back at me

6:45

Graduation day! As the realization washed over me, the excitement bubbled up inside. I had already showered the night before, freeing myself from the rush of the morning. Sitting up in bed, I took a moment to gather my thoughts and center myself.

"Today will be a good day, I know it will."

I closed my eyes and whispered a prayer, feeling the weight of this special day take root in my heart and nerves just a little bit.

"God, thank you for waking me up today," I said, feeling grateful for every breath and every moment. I asked for blessings on this day—to allow everything to go great and for the happiness of my family and friends to radiate around me. I thought back to the new shoes and clothes I had picked out, feeling thankful for those little joys too and making sure to mention those and thank god.

With my heart feeling lighter, I swung my legs over the side of the bed and made it, pulling the comforter tight and smoothing out the wrinkles while fluffing up my pillows. I took my phone off the charger and scrolled through my playlist.

"Let's start the day off great." I say to myself as I hit play on my favorite song. The familiar opening chords of "Country" by SZA filled the room, enveloping me in a warm embrace.

I'd always loved starting my mornings with her soothing voice; something about the melody and her ethereal tone made everything feel calm and bright. It was the perfect soundtrack to kick off such an important day.

After a blissful few moments lost in the mini dance battle against myself and my mirror, I headed to the bathroom to do my skin care. I splashed my face with warm water, feeling it wakes up my skin and wash the eye bags away, and then began brushing my teeth. I smiled as the familiar tune of One Direction started playing from my toothbrush. I got it from my grandma a month ago for getting straight A's on my report card and I haven't used another toothbrush since. My mom said you should change out your toothbrush every three months, so I was going to enjoy it as long as I could. My little quirky gadget that made dental hygiene much more enjoyable. I brushed along to the catchy lyrics, and when the music ceased after two minutes, I knew I had brushed long enough.

Once I finished, I carefully put on my outfit, sliding into my skirt and T-shirt. Looking in the mirror I grinned as I took off my bonnet, letting my hair fall free. With a brush in hand, I ran it through my hair, marveling at how well I'd managed to tame my hair, considering it's been straightened for two days and it still looked like it was the first day. Once my hair was the right amount of brushed and tamed, I reached for my favorite vanilla-scented lotion—my daily ritual. I love everything vanilla scented. The warm, sweet scent enveloped me, making my skin feel soft and hydrated. I spritzed on the matching vanilla perfume, making sure to hit all my pulse points, it was going to last all day.

Okay and now for the finishing touches, lip gloss. I pulled out my cherry scented clear lip gloss and applied a shimmering layer to my lips and admired my reflection in the mirror. My heart skipped a beat—I couldn't help but smile, I looked so nice and grown-ish. Like I was going to be a true middle schooler.

I took one last look in the mirror, satisfied with how everything came together. I grabbed my bag and headed downstairs. My dad was already there.

"Ready for the best day ever?" he asked, a wide smile plastered across his face.

"Absolutely!" I replied, practically bouncing in place.

"Okay perfect, we're going to get some Starbucks before I drop you guys off."

"YAY! Okay, perfect!" I shouted.

On the drive to Starbucks, Monney and I played Roblox, our favorite game of all time. Monney liked to play obby games, which was so hard. Well for me at least. You had to perfectly pass every obstacle or else you would die and have to start all the way over. It was so stupid. Like why do I have to start over when I was one jump away from the finish line? I will never understand it or why she liked it by hey, I was just happy to play with her.

We ended up compromising though when she realized the rage I was starting to have every time I died. We play three rounds of each game of each other and then trade off.

I think she was only being nice because it was graduation day, but you don't hear me complaining.

We got to Starbucks and placed our orders.

"May I please have a pink drink with extra strawberries?" I asked the barista.

"Yes of course. Anything else?"

"May I please have the same thing but with my strawberries." My sister added on with our drinks in hand, we talked and laughed about our plans for the day, soaking in the last serene moments before my graduation.

"I wish I could have a graduation so I didn't have to have a whole school day." Monney announced rolling her eyes,

"Aha, you're okay. Your mom is going to get you out of school early for Arri's graduation so you can watch." said dad

"YAY!!" Monney shouted but I didn't know if it was because she'll get me to watch me graduate or because she didn't have to stay for a full day of school… but I digress.

The car stopped in front of the school, and I glanced out the window. I grabbed my bag, slung it over my shoulder, and opened the door. The air was crisp, and the scent of freshly cut grass filled the morning. I could hear the chatter of kids ahead, already gathering at the school gate.

As I stepped out, I spotted her—Liyah, standing by the gate, her eyes lighting up when she saw me. She waved enthusiastically, and I couldn't help but smile back. There was something so comforting about seeing her this morning, like I was finally starting to believe that this was real—that we were really about to graduate. Monney friends appeared and she walked off with them, we hugged each other and went our separate ways.

"Are you ready for the best days of our lives?" Liyah asked as I walked up to her,

I nodded, trying to hide the butterflies in my stomach. "I guess so. It still doesn't feel real."

Liyah smirked, her eyes twinkling. "It's about to, trust me. Graduation's at 10:15, so we've got like two hours before everything goes down." She glanced around, as if the schoolyard was about to turn into a stage at any moment. "I can't wait to get this over with. I want to see you walk across that stage, looking all grown-up."

I laughed, shaking my head. "It's going to be weird. I'm going to miss everyone."

"I'll miss you the most," Liyah teased. "Even though we'll see each other like everyday during the summer or else I will hunt you down and kidnap you." she said laughing.

"Okay fair." I responded smiling.

She hugged me quickly, and then we both turned toward the entrance, chatting about everything and nothing at the same time.

"Where's Jay?" I asked, looking around.

"She's coming late, her mom bought donuts for the whole class—so, you know, priorities." She grinned, and I couldn't help but laugh. Typical Jay. I was just excited that I was getting Starbucks AND donuts all in one morning.

We headed inside, and the halls felt different today— emptier somehow, even though the buzz of excitement filled every corner. When we made it to our classroom, Mrs. G was waiting for us.

"Good morning, ladies and gentlemen. In about forty-five minutes, we all are going to head to the cafeteria to

I think she was only being nice because it was graduation day, but you don't hear me complaining.

We got to Starbucks and placed our orders.

"May I please have a pink drink with extra strawberries?" I asked the barista.

"Yes of course. Anything else?"

"May I please have the same thing but with my strawberries." My sister added on with our drinks in hand, we talked and laughed about our plans for the day, soaking in the last serene moments before my graduation.

"I wish I could have a graduation so I didn't have to have a whole school day." Monney announced rolling her eyes,

"Aha, you're okay. Your mom is going to get you out of school early for Arri's graduation so you can watch." said dad

"YAY!!" Monney shouted but I didn't know if it was because she'll get me to watch me graduate or because she didn't have to stay for a full day of school... but I digress.

The car stopped in front of the school, and I glanced out the window. I grabbed my bag, slung it over my shoulder, and opened the door. The air was crisp, and the scent of freshly cut grass filled the morning. I could hear the chatter of kids ahead, already gathering at the school gate.

As I stepped out, I spotted her—Liyah, standing by the gate, her eyes lighting up when she saw me. She waved enthusiastically, and I couldn't help but smile back. There was something so comforting about seeing her this morning, like I was finally starting to believe that this was real—that we were really about to graduate. Monney friends appeared and she walked off with them, we hugged each other and went our separate ways.

"Are you ready for the best days of our lives?" Liyah asked as I walked up to her,

I nodded, trying to hide the butterflies in my stomach. "I guess so. It still doesn't feel real."

Liyah smirked, her eyes twinkling. "It's about to, trust me. Graduation's at 10:15, so we've got like two hours before everything goes down." She glanced around, as if the schoolyard was about to turn into a stage at any moment. "I can't wait to get this over with. I want to see you walk across that stage, looking all grown-up."

I laughed, shaking my head. "It's going to be weird. I'm going to miss everyone."

"I'll miss you the most," Liyah teased. "Even though we'll see each other like everyday during the summer or else I will hunt you down and kidnap you." she said laughing.

"Okay fair." I responded smiling.

She hugged me quickly, and then we both turned toward the entrance, chatting about everything and nothing at the same time.

"Where's Jay?" I asked, looking around.

"She's coming late, her mom bought donuts for the whole class—so, you know, priorities." She grinned, and I couldn't help but laugh. Typical Jay. I was just excited that I was getting Starbucks AND donuts all in one morning.

We headed inside, and the halls felt different today—emptier somehow, even though the buzz of excitement filled every corner. When we made it to our classroom, Mrs. G was waiting for us.

"Good morning, ladies and gentlemen. In about forty-five minutes, we all are going to head to the cafeteria to prepare for the ceremony but before then I have just a few words I would like to say.

"You all have come so far," Mrs. G started, standing in front of us with a proud smile. "I'm so proud of each and every one of you. You've worked so hard, and I know that no matter what you do, you will all achieve greatness. You'll be whatever it is you dream of being, and I can't wait to see all the amazing things you'll do in the future."

Her words hit me harder than I expected, and I could feel my eyes starting to tear up. We had all been together for so long, and now we were about to head in different directions, but Mrs. G's speech reminded me that we were ready. We had made it.

After some time, all the fifth-grade classes filed into the cafeteria to begin organizing the ceremony. The rows had already been lined up last night, so I knew I wouldn't be standing next to Liyah or Jay because our last names were far apart from each other, but it was okay. We were all in this together, even if we weren't physically side-by-side.

"Okay so we're going to just do a practice ceremony, make sure all you guys know where you're going and where you're going to stand. Everyone will shake the principal's hand and take a quick picture with her and then step down to their spot." Said the assistant principal.

After what felt like five minutes, it was time for the real ceremony. We all sat in our assigned seats, waving to our parents as we watched them slowly come in with balloons and some even with cakes.

My mom and dad came first and later on my grandparents, all with balloons and candy in their hands.

"Good morning, Parents and Guardians! The day we all have been waiting for is finally here. The day your children take the next big step of their life. The fear of the unknown but the joy of approaching it. I would like to thank each and every one of you for raising such amazing kids. Kids who have shown love, kindness, respect and honesty. Everything we can ask for! Now I know you guys are ready for your kids to get their certificate so I'll stop talking so much and get into the ceremony!!"

Everyone laughed and the ceremony began.

I tried to focus on the ceremony itself, but my mind kept wandering. The moment felt surreal— knowing any moment I will be walking across that stage, hearing my name called, and seeing my family in the crowd with their proud, teary eyes. It was like the day had been set in slow motion, every second stretching out into a beautiful memory I would carry with me forever.

Thank you, Mrs. H class of 2018! Now Mrs. G class…

My heart was pumping so fast, it's like it went so fast. I didn't even hear June's or Lila's name being called. I just remember my eyes watering and my hands clapping and as soon as I realized what was happening, my name was called.

"Arrionna Wright!!"

I felt frozen in time, a rush of pride came across me as I got up and walked across the stage, the applause and screams from my parents and family echoing in my ears. Mrs. G handed me my certificate, and I couldn't help but smile at her, as if she was silently telling me everything would be okay.

I wasn't just graduating; I was stepping into a new chapter. And somehow, that made everything feel a little more possible.

I stood up and walked over to the stage. It felt like I took 5000 steps to get there. As soon as my foot touched the stage, I could hear my family's loud screams and cheers. Even my sister was yelling "Sissy, Sissy." It felt so surreal.

"Congratulations Arrionna." The principal said as she shook my hand and handed me my diploma. I walked over to Mrs. G and immediately tears filled my eyes. She was more than a teacher; she was a friend and a mentor. An inspiration. She was family.

"I'm forever proud of you Arrionna, may this next chapter in your life bring you nothing but joy, peace and love." she whispered to me as she held me tight. Neither of us wanted to let go but we knew that we had to and so we did

After the ceremony was over, we all gathered with our families for pictures, and I couldn't hold back my smile as I saw my parents getting choked up, their tears mixing with their pride. My dad kept shaking his head, muttering how "time flies," and my mom kept hugging me over and over, like she couldn't believe this day had come. After two thousand pictures, we were ready to leave the school. My grandparents gave me one last hug and headed home. They reminded me at least 30 times before they left how proud of me they were and said how they knew one day I was going to make history. I laughed them off and waved them goodbye as they drove away from my school.

"Okay enough happy tears, I'm starving. What are we feeling like?" said my dad.

"Ouu I have a special place in mind, can I type it into the GPS? I asked my dad."

"Go ahead kid, it's your day!"

After about 10 minutes or so we arrived at our destination. AKA the best place in the world.

"APPLEBEES!" I chanted as I got out of the car.

"Aha I should've known, Applebees" my parents said laughing. I love how good they were at being parents. Even though they weren't together, both of them always made sure they were there for my sister and I and never made us feel like we were some objects that they had to fight over time for.

As soon as we walked into the restaurant the smell of sizzling shrimp and the warm, cozy atmosphere hit me instantly, and I couldn't wait to dig into my usual order—shrimp, chicken, mashed potatoes, and mushrooms.

"Mushrooms are the best thing that's ever come onto the earth," I said with a grin, digging into my plate.

My dad chuckled from across the table. "You always say that. But hey, I'm not arguing." He picked up his fork, and we all continued eating, chatting about the day and what was coming next.

After lunch, my dad took us to the mall and my mom went home. She was really tired from work. We went on a mini shopping spree, picking out a few new outfits for the summer, and I even treated myself to a new pair of sneakers, well my dad did but still. We joked around, walking through the aisles and laughing over the weirdest things, everything just felt... perfect.

Later that night, I curled up on the couch with my family, ready to end the day with something fun. We picked a scary

I wasn't just graduating; I was stepping into a new chapter. And somehow, that made everything feel a little more possible.

I stood up and walked over to the stage. It felt like I took 5000 steps to get there. As soon as my foot touched the stage, I could hear my family's loud screams and cheers. Even my sister was yelling "Sissy, Sissy." It felt so surreal.

"Congratulations Arrionna." The principal said as she shook my hand and handed me my diploma. I walked over to Mrs. G and immediately tears filled my eyes. She was more than a teacher; she was a friend and a mentor. An inspiration. She was family.

"I'm forever proud of you Arrionna, may this next chapter in your life bring you nothing but joy, peace and love." she whispered to me as she held me tight. Neither of us wanted to let go but we knew that we had to and so we did

After the ceremony was over, we all gathered with our families for pictures, and I couldn't hold back my smile as I saw my parents getting choked up, their tears mixing with their pride. My dad kept shaking his head, muttering how "time flies," and my mom kept hugging me over and over, like she couldn't believe this day had come. After two thousand pictures, we were ready to leave the school. My grandparents gave me one last hug and headed home. They reminded me at least 30 times before they left how proud of me they were and said how they knew one day I was going to make history. I laughed them off and waved them goodbye as they drove away from my school.

"Okay enough happy tears, I'm starving. What are we feeling like?" said my dad.

"Ouu I have a special place in mind, can I type it into the GPS? I asked my dad."

"Go ahead kid, it's your day!"

After about 10 minutes or so we arrived at our destination. AKA the best place in the world.

"APPLEBEES!" I chanted as I got out of the car.

"Aha I should've known, Applebees" my parents said laughing. I love how good they were at being parents. Even though they weren't together, both of them always made sure they were there for my sister and I and never made us feel like we were some objects that they had to fight over time for.

As soon as we walked into the restaurant the smell of sizzling shrimp and the warm, cozy atmosphere hit me instantly, and I couldn't wait to dig into my usual order—shrimp, chicken, mashed potatoes, and mushrooms.

"Mushrooms are the best thing that's ever come onto the earth," I said with a grin, digging into my plate.

My dad chuckled from across the table. "You always say that. But hey, I'm not arguing." He picked up his fork, and we all continued eating, chatting about the day and what was coming next.

After lunch, my dad took us to the mall and my mom went home. She was really tired from work. We went on a mini shopping spree, picking out a few new outfits for the summer, and I even treated myself to a new pair of sneakers, well my dad did but still. We joked around, walking through the aisles and laughing over the weirdest things, everything just felt... perfect.

Later that night, I curled up on the couch with my family, ready to end the day with something fun. We picked a scary movie—because why not? I loved scary movies, well unless it was satanic ones… then you couldn't catch me watching those ever. Those were too extreme so we picked a thriller.

The house was quiet, the lights were off, and the flickering of the TV screen was the only thing breaking the silence. I buried my face in a blanket during the most intense parts of the movie, but I couldn't stop laughing at how much my dad jumped at the jump scares.

As the movie ended, I couldn't help but think how different everything would be tomorrow. I was officially a graduate, ready to start summer break, and yet, it all felt so unreal. But one thing was for sure: I would never forget this day, and I knew that the best was yet to come.

And as I laid down that night, drifting off to sleep with the sound of my family's voices in the background, I knew that, somehow, this was just the beginning.

Chapter 6

Summer Vacation

Yes, finally. Day one with no school! Life was great. I already had three back-to-back dreams about all the fun stuff I was going to do this summer. Well, they were all about swimming, but regardless, it was summer! I was going to have the perfect summer before I headed into Junior High, where new teachers and more responsibility loomed ahead like a distant wave. This summer was mine to seize, filled with possibilities, and I was determined to make the most of it.

Later that day, I heard my phone vibrate on the kitchen counter. I grabbed it, a surge of excitement coursing through me as I saw it was a message from my friends Liyah and Jay. They wanted to hang out that very day and go get frozen yogurt. "Yes!" I thought to myself. I typed back quickly with an enthusiastic "Of course! What time?"

As the day wore on, the heat began to rise, making my hair puffier than usual, like a dandelion caught in a summer breeze. My mom noticed and offered to help. With deft fingers, she braided my hair into two quick, neat plaits that lay against my shoulders, and I admired the way they almost swung as I moved.

I rummaged through my closet, finally pulling out my favorite pair of Old Navy jeans. They were just the right combination of comfort and style, their faded hue a perfect match for the summer vibe. Feeling nostalgic, I couldn't help but remember the numerous adventures I had shared in those jeans. But as I caught a glimpse of the tear down by the leg, I came to the reluctant realization that it might finally be time to find a new pair. "Maybe next week," I told myself as I shrugged on a light, airy tank top. The outfit was complete, and I headed out, my heart racing with anticipation.

Meeting up with Liyah and Jay at the local froyo shop felt like stepping into the best part of summer. The air was fragrant with sugary softness, and the counter was lined with a vibrant array of frosty flavors—everything from classic vanilla to exotic taro. As we waited in line, we debated which toppings would reign supreme on our concoctions. Sprinkles? Fruit? There was something exhilarating about these simple decisions when they were paired with laughter and excitement.

After we grabbed our yummy treats, we headed outside to find a spot under a giant oak tree, its branches providing shade from the sun's glaring rays. We dug into our froyo, and our conversation flowed effortlessly, oscillating between the latest TikTok trends and the joys of endless summer days. Liyah insisted that we should plan a trip to the water park nearby, while Jay was keen on organizing a sleepover at his place to watch all the latest movies. The plans we spun seemed limitless; each suggestion more thrilling than the last.

When I got home that evening, full of froyo and laughter, I realized summer was already shaping up to be everything I had hoped for. I knew these moments mattered, that they would become memories woven into the fabric of my youth. The anticipation for junior high began to fade as I embraced the present, the sweetness of the day lingering like the last drops of my melty frozen yogurt.

◆

The next day came quickly, waking to the sun streaming through my window, inviting me to rise and embrace all the possibilities ahead. My phone buzzed again, this time with a string of messages from Liyah and Jay. They wanted to meet up again, this time for a bike ride around the neighborhood. "Let's make it an adventure!" Liyah suggested with a series of emojis that made me chuckle.

I grabbed my bike from the garage, dusting off a few cobwebs that had formed over the winter. My bike, named Blue Lightning, had seen many adventures, from neighborhood races to long rides to the park. I swiftly packed a small backpack with water bottles and snacks—because what's an adventure without sustenance? With my hair now pulled back into a high ponytail, I felt ready for whatever the day would throw my way.

We met at the park, the air warm and buzzing with the sounds of children playing and birds chirping. The three of us mounted our bikes and set off, riding along the winding paths that threaded through the trees. The breeze cooled us off as we pedaled faster, racing to the small pond at the far end of the park.

Once we arrived, Liyah suggested we have a mini picnic by the water; what better to accompany our bike ride than some tasty snacks? We spread out a patchwork blanket we found buried in Jay's backpack, munching on granola bars, fruit, and those beloved gummy bears that always seemed to bring an extra hint of joy.

We hung out by the pond, laughing and joking, sharing stories of our favorite summer memories from the past, and crafting outrageous plans for what we could do next. As the sun began to set, painting the sky in a gradient of oranges and pinks, I felt a flicker of gratitude wash over me.

The bond we shared felt deeper than school friendships; this was a summer friendship, airy and free, unencumbered by the pressures of grades and tests. As twilight settled, I felt a sense of belonging, a realization that these moments were the true essence of youth.

As day two of summer came to a close, with the world bathed in the warm glow of dusk, I couldn't help but smile. I was ready to soak up every moment until that first day of junior high, every adventure with Liyah and Jay serving as a reminder that before the demands of growing up settled in, there was a whole season of blissful simplicity and joy awaiting me. Summer had only just begun, and I had a feeling it would be one for the ages.

"Good morning!" screamed my dad. "Time to get up." He said, shaking my sister and I up out of our sleep.

"Ugh, what time is it?" my sister sighed.

"Oh just 6am."

Um so did I hear that right? 6am?? Hello?

"Dad, why are we up at 6am?" I replied in confusion, still wiping the eye boogers out of my eyes.

"You guys are getting older and need to start instilling good habits within yourself to grow into productive, smart and healthy women. So we are going to start running at the high school track field by the house every weekday at 6am. Then after we're going to get some books and read, and I signed you guys up for this summer tutoring math program. It helps keep you guys sharp while you're out of school because taking a break for two months is a very long time. Then after whatever fun or video games you guys want to play, you can."

I mean I wasn't completely opposed to the idea. It sounded fun. I didn't mind running when the sun was first rising. It would be so pretty and doing something productive to start off your day always sets the atmosphere for the day.. Now my sister Monney on the other hand.. Oh she hated the idea.

"WHY THE HAY IS HE WAKING US UP AT 6AM TO RUNN!" "I mean don't get me wrong, starting off your day with a wonderful outdoor activity sounds wonderful, I'm all for it but when I wake up.. You know.. PAST 9 O'clock!

"Yeah but then it would be super hot." I tell her laughing as we brush our teeth besides each other.

"I don't even care. As long as I got my full 9 hours and food, I'd take anything I could get, but 6am is absolutely absurd. "

I laughed at her, brushing her off and grabbed my phone to text our group chat.

"Good morning, guys! I know you guys are probably wondering why I'm up at the crack of dawn aha. My dad has me doing this new productive routine and I mean hey I'm willing to try it out soo but love you guys! Hope you're sleeping amazing."

"You guys ready my dad

shouted from downstairs. "We're gonna leave in five minutes!"

I couldn't help but roll my eyes. My dad was so determined to get us on a "productive" schedule. It was like he had a whole new agenda for us that involved zero sleep and way more running. I mean, I get it, he wanted the best for us, but 6 AM every day? That was pushing it.

"Coming, Dad!" I yelled back as I finished brushing my teeth. I glanced at Monney, who was still slumped against the bathroom door with a look of total defeat.

"You're doing this because you want to make sure I'm not the only one suffering, aren't you?" she muttered, barely able to keep her eyes open.

"Of course, it's all about equality," I joked, but deep down, I knew she wasn't wrong. I mean, I wasn't thrilled either, but maybe the fresh air and quiet morning would be nice.

We both trudged downstairs to find Dad already putting on his running shoes, looking like he'd just finished a marathon. He was so chipper about everything, it made me feel like I was the one slacking off. I glanced at Monney, who was still trying to keep her eyelids from closing.

By the time we made it to the high school track, the sun had just started to peek over the horizon, casting an orange glow on the pavement. The track was completely empty, which was kind of nice. I always felt like the world was asleep except for us, like we were the only ones doing something with our time. I looked over at Monney, who was already dragging her feet as she made her way onto the track.

Dad stretched his arms in the air, trying to motivate us. "We're going to run a few laps today to get those legs moving. No excuses!"

I gave a half-hearted nod and started running with Monney beside me, though we were both going way slower than Dad. He had that annoying ability to run and make it look effortless, like it was a breeze for him. Meanwhile, I felt like I might pass out after just half a lap. Monney, on the other hand, was practically crawling.

We finished our laps eventually, but it wasn't because we were fast or determined — it was because Dad kept shouting encouragement from the sidelines, and we didn't want to disappoint him.

When we finally stopped, gasping for air, Monney and I flopped onto the grass. I could barely move my legs, but there was a weird sense of accomplishment.

Dad didn't even break a sweat. "Good job, girls! You're gonna feel so much better once you get into the routine of this!"

"Yeah, yeah," Monney grumbled, wiping sweat off her forehead. "You're gonna feel better when you let us sleep in for once."

"Not gonna happen," Dad said, laughing as he grabbed his water bottle. "Now let's go grab those books and hit the library!"

Over the next few days, I fell into a strange rhythm. It was starting to feel like a pattern I couldn't break, a machine I was part of but couldn't escape My mornings became something of a routine: 6 AM wake-up, a quick breakfast that I knew was good for me but felt like a chore to eat, followed by the run at the high school track, and then the trip to the library. Slowly, the discomfort of early mornings started to fade, replaced by a kind of grudging acceptance. I still wasn't a fan of the early wake-ups, but I began to see that they were making me feel a little more accomplished.

Breakfast had turned into a major production, all thanks to Dad's insistence on "filling up with protein." He was obsessed with making sure we were "fueling up" the right way, which, for him, meant eggs, sausage, oatmeal with protein powder mixed in, and a glass of milk. I usually hated the combination of eggs and oatmeal, but Dad was all about the nutritional value, so I learned to choke it down.

I started looking at food differently. I didn't just eat to fill the hunger; I ate to "build" my body. At least, that's what Dad kept telling me. "Protein is the building block of muscle," he'd remind me while he scarfed down his own breakfast, always finishing first and then offering a well-timed, "Keep up, girls!" It became this little challenge: could I eat it all before the clock hit 6:30?

Monney would whine and complain as she picked at her eggs, rolling her eyes every time Dad came in with a new set of "rules" for us to follow. But I didn't mind. It was hard to argue with the benefits that came from eating all this protein, especially since my running was starting to feel less like torture. My legs felt stronger, and when I would finish my laps on the track, I no longer felt like I was going to collapse in a heap.

And honestly, after a few weeks, I started to notice some changes. It wasn't just in how my legs felt stronger, or how I could run faster than I used to, but also in how my body felt—more awake, more energized. Even Monney started to complain less. Not that she was a fan, but the first time she managed to finish a full lap without stopping, I saw a glimmer of pride in her eyes, even if she wouldn't admit it out loud.

By the time we got to the library, my body was buzzing from all the protein and movement, but my mind was still sluggish. The thing that really caught me off guard was the math tutoring Dad had signed us up for. I wasn't particularly excited about it. Math had always been my weakest subject. I could do the basics, but when it came to algebra and geometry, I would just zone out, feeling like I was drowning in a sea of numbers and equations.

But then something started happening.

It wasn't a magical moment where everything clicked at once, but I began to notice that the problems started making more sense as I worked through them. I wasn't solving equations instantly, but I could follow the steps. The tutoring sessions, which initially felt like a waste of time, suddenly became something I looked forward to.

I remember sitting at the library one day, halfway through a worksheet on quadratic equations, when I realized I was actually understanding it. I sat back in my chair, surprised at myself. It wasn't perfect—I still had moments where I got stuck—but the fact that I was even making progress was a huge win for me.

"What do you think about this one?" I asked Monney, pointing at a particularly difficult equation. She shot me an exhausted look.

"I'm not even going to try. You know math is like a foreign language to me. Good luck with that, though."

But that was okay. I wasn't doing it for her approval, I was doing it for myself.

Dad had always told us that working hard now would pay off in the future. He'd even explained that math wasn't just about numbers but about learning how to think logically. I'd never really believed him until I found myself solving problems without feeling completely overwhelmed by them.

Each day after our tutoring sessions, we'd head home, and I'd tackle the same routine: eating a hefty lunch full of protein—usually grilled chicken, vegetables, and more eggs—then maybe some downtime where I could just relax before diving into the math problems again. Some days, I would catch myself re-reading the concepts from the tutoring session, making sure I had a solid grasp on them.

By the fourth week, I noticed how much my body was changing. I wasn't exactly shredded or anything, but I had more muscle tone than I ever had before. My arms were more defined, and my legs felt like they were built for running—like I could go for miles if I really tried. I was stronger, both physically and mentally.

Monney still grumbled every time we had to go to tutoring, but she was getting better at math too, just in her own way. Though she never fully embraced the whole "productive routine" Dad had set up, she at least tolerated it. When we would compare our math answers later, we'd occasionally get into little debates over how to solve something, but I had to admit, there was a bit of a rivalry brewing. Monney and I would tease each other about our tutoring progress, each of us trying to get the upper hand. It was nice to have that little spark of competition, something to lighten the heavy atmosphere that Dad's routine had created.

But despite all of this—my body changing, my math comprehension was improving, and the fact that I was starting to feel like I could actually keep up—something felt off. The more I focused on improving myself, the more I realized I was drifting further away from my friends. The group chat felt quieter and quieter, and when I tried to bring up my daily routine, it didn't seem to spark any interest in them. I didn't want to seem like I was rubbing it in their faces, but every time I'd mention how I was feeling a little more confident or how I finally understood a tough math concept, the responses I got were short, almost dismissive.

One day, as I was walking back from the library after another productive math session, I decided to text the group again. I needed to know if anyone had noticed the changes in me—or if I was just imagining it.

"Hey guys, how's everyone doing? I've been running and doing some extra math lately, and I feel like I'm getting stronger... mentally and physically. It's kind of cool."

Ellie replied almost immediately, but her response was not what I was hoping for: "That's cool. We've been kind of busy with other things. Anyway, I'm sure you'll keep improving."

I stared at the message for a long time, feeling a pang of loneliness that seemed to grow larger with each passing day. Was this really it? Was this the path I was on now?

Dad, on the other hand, seemed oblivious to the growing distance between me and my friends. Every day, he would ask me how my tutoring went, if I was getting better at my running, and even if I felt stronger. And every time, I gave him an honest answer, even though a small part of me wished for the companionship I used to have with my friends.

But at least I had my routine. My dad's insistence on all these new habits had given me structure when I felt like everything else in my life was falling apart. It was just that now, it wasn't just the early mornings or the math that kept me busy—it was the nagging feeling that I was losing something, something important.

The next few weeks followed the same pattern. Every morning, we were up at 6 AM, running and then heading to the library to pick out new books. I never got used to the early mornings, but I figured maybe it wasn't *that* bad. I did feel a little more productive, even though Monney and I would spend the majority of our time at the library joking around rather than reading.

But something weird started happening around the third week.

It wasn't the usual carefree summer vibe I had been used to. I hadn't heard much from my friends in the group chat, which wasn't abnormal for a few days, but then days turned into weeks. I thought maybe they were just busy, or maybe I was missing out on some group hangouts, but the silence was loud. Every time I texted them, it was like I was being ignored.

"Hey, guys, what's up? Miss you all!" I messaged in the group chat, hoping to get some attention.

The responses were sparse, and when they did come, they felt off.

"Heyyy, sorry! Been busy. How's the whole 6 AM thing going? Lol." That was from Ellie, the usually bubbly one.

"Good luck with that, I guess. I'm just gonna sleep through the summer, lol."

That was the last message I got from her.

Then there was Noah. He didn't respond at all.

At first, I shrugged it off, thinking they were just all caught up in their own stuff. But as days passed, it became painfully obvious. I would text the group chat, and the messages would get more and more ignored. I was left on read, which felt even worse than not getting a reply at all.

One day, I decided to call Ellie. I hadn't heard from her in over a week, and I missed our usual chats.

She picked up on the third ring. "Hey, what's up?"

"Hey, I've been texting the group chat, but no one's responding to me. Is everything okay?"

There was a long pause on the other end. "Yeah, everything's fine. Just been... busy with stuff, you know? Summer's been kinda crazy."

I didn't buy it. "Busy with what? You never mentioned anything."

"Just... stuff, you know?" She said it again, like I was supposed to get it. "Look, I gotta go. Talk to you later."

The call ended abruptly.

I stared at my phone, my stomach sinking. It didn't take a genius to figure out something had shifted. They were avoiding me. But why?

The next day, I went on social media to check what everyone was up to. I saw that they were hanging out without me—posting pictures at the beach, playing games, going out for ice cream. Everything seemed so normal for them, but I wasn't a part of it anymore.

I tried to reach out again. "Hey, guys, what's going on? I haven't heard from you in forever."

Noah was the only one who replied, but his message was short and distant: "Hey, sorry. We've just been kind of hanging out. Hope everything's good with you."

Everything felt off. I could tell they were all drifting away from me. It hurt more than I thought it would. At first, I couldn't understand what had changed. I thought maybe I was too focused on my dad's schedule and had been too distant. But the more I thought about it, the more I realized: they just weren't that interested anymore.

I started to feel like an outsider in my own group of friends.

It wasn't just the group chat anymore. In person, they seemed different too. When I saw them at the store, they'd wave and give me a half-hearted smile, but there was no warmth, no excitement to see me. It was like they were going through the motions.

One day, I ran into Ellie and Noah at the local cafe. It was one of those awkward run-ins where you know they didn't expect to see you. I tried to start a conversation, but it felt forced. They were laughing about something I didn't get, and when I tried to join in, the silence that followed was deafening.

"Um, I should go," Ellie said, standing up and grabbing her things. "We're meeting up with some other people."

It was like a punch to the gut.

And that was the beginning of the end. My friends had slowly started ignoring me, and no matter how hard I tried to reach out, nothing seemed to work. Maybe they had grown tired of me. Or maybe I had just changed too much. Either way, the bond that used to feel so strong was now unraveling, and I was left wondering what happened to the friendship I had taken for granted.

Days turned into weeks, and I began to spend more time with my dad. At least he wasn't going anywhere. At least he still cared. I couldn't say the same about my friends.

After weeks of early mornings, running, and tutoring, I finally got a break from Dad's strict routine. We were going on a family trip to California. The idea of taking a break felt like a breath of fresh air, and even though I had fallen into the groove of my new life, I welcomed the change of scenery.

The trip was something Dad had been planning for months, and the excitement in his voice when he talked about it made me smile. "It'll be a great time for the whole family to get away," he'd say, looking over maps of the places we'd visit. But I wasn't as excited as I should have been. California sounded amazing, of course—sunny beaches, cool vibes, and scenic hikes—but the trip also made me nervous. I hadn't seen my friends in weeks, and the idea of being away from everything familiar felt odd. I wasn't sure what I'd find when I returned.

We flew out from the airport early in the morning, a 5 AM flight that had me groggily waking up long before the sun. Dad was practically bouncing off the walls, making sure we were packed and ready. My sister Monney, however, looked like she was still asleep, her head lolling to the side as she slouched in her seat at the gate. We finally boarded the plane, and the moment I sat down, I tried to get comfortable, settling in with my headphones, hoping to catch a few hours of sleep before the fun began.

The plane ride was uneventful. I tried to distract myself with my phone, scrolling through social media, but I quickly grew tired of the endless stream of posts from friends I hadn't spoken to in forever. I closed the app and stared out the window, letting my mind wander. The clouds outside looked endless, and I couldn't help but feel like I was leaving something behind as we flew further away from home.

When we finally landed in California, the warm air hit me like a wall. It was nothing like the humid mornings we had back home. This air was dry and clean, and I couldn't help but breathe it in deeply, savoring the difference. We hopped into the rental car and drove toward our first stop—Los Angeles. The city looked even more vibrant than I'd imagined, the sun casting a golden glow over everything. The palm trees were everywhere, and the skyline seemed to stretch on forever. I couldn't help but marvel at the massive buildings and the strange mix of people bustling around.

We drove through Hollywood, and Dad was practically bursting with enthusiasm as he pointed out landmarks. "That's the Hollywood sign! Oh, and that's where the Oscars are held!" he said, practically jumping out of his seat with excitement. Monney and I didn't really share his enthusiasm—she was too busy taking selfies with exaggerated poses and a bored expression, while I half-listened, caught up in the bustle around me.

Our first stop was Venice Beach. Dad was determined to soak in every inch of California, so he insisted we go for a walk along the pier. As we walked, I noticed how different everything felt. The pace was slower, and people seemed relaxed and carefree. I spotted a few skateboarders zooming by, effortlessly carving through the crowded street, their board wheels clicking against the pavement like a rhythm I didn't quite understand but envied.

We spent hours at the beach, the salty air filling my lungs as I sat in the sand, letting the waves crash against my legs. I could feel my tension melt away with each wave. There was something so simple and freeing about being by the ocean. The sound of seagulls overhead, the distant chatter of tourists, and the soft sand beneath my feet—it was a world away from the early mornings and the endless routine I'd been following back home. For a while, I let myself be absorbed in the experience, not thinking about the things I had been struggling with—my friends, my increasingly rigid lifestyle, or the loneliness I hadn't been able to shake.

As the sun began to set, painting the sky with shades of pink and orange, we walked along the boardwalk, where street performers played music and people sold handmade jewelry. Monney bought a cheap necklace from one of the vendors, and I picked up a hand-painted postcard of the beach to send to a friend, although I wasn't sure who that would be yet.

The next day, we drove up to Malibu, where the drive was scenic and breathtaking. The winding roads took us high above the cliffs, giving us a view of the ocean that seemed to go on forever. I leaned my head against the window, gazing out at the waves crashing against the rocks below. It felt like a dream, the kind of place I'd only seen in movies. We stopped at a little restaurant overlooking the ocean for lunch, and I watched surfers riding the waves while we ate fresh seafood and tacos.

The food was incredible. I ordered fish tacos, and I swear they were the best I had ever had. There was something about the way the seafood tasted so fresh, combined with the tang of lime and the slight crunch of the tortilla. I realized how much I'd been missing out on the simple pleasures of food—back home, I had been so focused on protein-heavy meals that I'd forgotten how enjoyable a good meal could be. In California, it felt like eating was an experience, not just a fuel to get through the day.

After lunch, we drove to Santa Monica Pier. The boardwalk was bustling with people, and the energy was contagious. I was finally starting to feel like I was escaping the weight of my routine. We walked around, visited the arcade, and even got on a Ferris wheel that overlooked the beach. From up there, everything looked so small and far away, and for the first time in a long time, I felt a sense of freedom I hadn't felt in weeks.

Monney and I argued playfully over who would win at the claw machine, and I ended up winning a stuffed bear. I couldn't help but laugh as I held it in my arms, the simple joy of the moment creeping in, reminding me of what it felt like to truly be present.

That night, we stayed at a hotel near the beach. The air was cooler by then, and we sat on the balcony, watching the lights of the city twinkle in the distance. I couldn't help but reflect on how much had changed since the trip had started. The weight of everything I'd been carrying—the loneliness, the pressure to maintain this "perfect" routine—seemed to lift a little. California was a fresh start, even if just for a moment.

The trip wasn't just about the places we visited—it was about the way I started to let go. I realized that, for the first time in weeks, I wasn't measuring my progress in miles run or math problems solved. I was just experiencing life. It felt like the most freeing thing I'd done in a long time.

By the end of the trip, I felt like I had learned something important. I had spent so much time focusing on my personal growth that I had forgotten how to truly live in the moment. But in California, I rediscovered that balance. I wasn't just running or solving problems anymore—I was letting myself enjoy life again, one sunset at a time.

The flight back from California was a much-needed chance for me to finally rest. After a week of constant activity—early mornings, sightseeing, and constant movement—my body felt heavy with exhaustion. The airplane seat was surprisingly comfortable, and the moment I sat down, I immediately sank into the plush fabric, feeling the weight of the past few days finally catch up with me. My body was sore from all the walking and exploring, and my eyes were tired from taking in all the new sights and sounds. As the plane took off and we ascended into the sky, I let out a long breath and leaned my head back against the seat, closing my eyes.

The sound of the plane's engines humming in the background made me feel oddly peaceful. The exhaustion from the trip was overwhelming, and for the first time in days, I allowed myself to drift into a deep, uninterrupted sleep. I don't even remember when I fell asleep—I just know that I woke up, startled, when the seatbelt sign came on as the plane began its descent.

I rubbed my eyes and blinked several times to shake off the fogginess. For a brief moment, I felt disoriented, not sure whether I was still in California or back in the reality I had left behind. I glanced out of the window, spotting the city's skyline beneath the blanket of clouds. It was strange, but in a way, I missed the simplicity of the beach and the carefreeness of California. The plane ride home felt like the last piece of that vacation, almost like I was taking one last breath of the freedom I'd experienced before returning to my routine.

The flight attendants came by with snacks, but I wasn't hungry. The heavy meals I had been eating over the past few days in California were still sitting in my stomach, reminding me that I needed to eat less when I got home. Dad was already reading his book, and Monney was staring at her phone, scrolling through photos of all the things we'd done. It was odd to think about how quickly the trip had passed, like it was this perfect snapshot of time that I could never quite get back.

As the plane touched down and we taxied to the gate, I couldn't help but feel a little sad. I hadn't realized it while I was there, but California had been a release—a chance to escape the rigid routine I had locked myself into. It had been a space where I could breathe freely and just live. But now, as the plane came to a stop and the reality of what awaited me back home crept in, I was filled with a mix of anticipation and dread.

I collected my things and filed off the plane with my family, dragging my feet a little more than usual. The world outside felt so different after the week I had spent away. It was almost as if I had to recalibrate myself back into my life—back into the routine of morning runs, math tutoring, and the never-ending focus on being "productive."

When we got home, everything was still the same, and yet everything felt different. My room was just how I had left it—untidy but comfortable, familiar—but there was a new heaviness to it. I couldn't exactly place what had shifted, but I felt it in my chest, like I was carrying something I couldn't define. Maybe it was the weight of being back in the same place, where everything had once felt so easy. Maybe it was the feeling that, somehow, I had changed while I was away—and not just physically, but emotionally too.

I dropped my bags on my bed and plopped down beside them, grabbing my phone to check for any messages. As I scrolled through my notifications, my thumb paused over a text message that caught my eye.

It was from Lila.

"Hey. uh wyd?"

My heart skipped a beat as I read the message. It had been weeks since I last heard from her. The silence between us had felt like a slow drift, like she was moving on without me. But this message, it was like a lifeline thrown into the stillness.

I quickly typed a reply, my fingers moving faster than I expected them to.

"Hey! I missed you. I just got back from California—had such a great time, now I'm going back to my moms house. I've been missing all the usual stuff we used to do. How have you been?"

As I hit send, I suddenly felt a little nervous. I wasn't sure what to expect, but I was hoping this would be a chance to reconnect. Maybe this would be the start of us picking up where we left off, before all the running and tutoring and changes took over.

It didn't take long before Lila replied, and when I saw her message pop up, I couldn't help but grin.

"California? That sounds amazing! I'm so glad you got to go. Things have been good on my end, just super busy hanging out with friends. Can we talk?"

I let out a breath I didn't realize I'd been holding.

"Sure, What's up?"

I spent the next few minutes staring at the screen, wondering what we needed to talk about? Maybe the next hang out? We can sort my seashells that I collected and maybe try to make paper copies. She loved art and crafts.

Before I could overthink it even more, I got another message from her.

"Arri I'm sorry to have to tell you this but June and I don't want to be your friend anymore. Maybe it's because we're not in elementary school anymore or something but we're just growing into different people. Well, I guess what I mean is, you just seem so boring now. June and I hang out every day, that's what true besties do. You just like to stay at home all day, worrying about some classes that you aren't even in until 2 months from now. You're working out like you're training for the Olympics or something? It's like you think you're "too grown" for us now. We don't really like you anymore. Not in a "ew your gross and we hate you" way, but more like you're just not for us anymore. I'm sorry... duos are easier anyways. You'll find some other friends, I know it! Love you lots."

I stared at the gray message on my screen and immediately tears filled my eyes. Thousands of words flooded my mind but seconds later disappeared and came back again in spurs. The only thought my brain decided to focus on was the thought of being alone. The thought that I was so easily disposable and replaceable to the people I thought loved me.

I hovered my hands over my keyboard. Hoping to type something, anything that will fix this. Should I beg them not to leave? June didn't even bother texting me, she was probably with Lila right at that moment.

Should I tell them that I will change for them? That I'll start hanging out with them more. Making myself available to them whenever. I'll drop some of my summer classes for them, I know those take up a lot of time and no one wants to be friends with a worrier. Someone who's always stressed. I'll compromise myself for them. Anything to keep them around. I could always run whenever. Whenever I was done hanging out with them.

My hands finally unfroze and I was able to type.

"Wait." I sent.

My finger fluttered over my keys and I began to type some more.

"Please don't. I understand that I've been busy and focused too much on school. It's summer and I should be with my best friends. You guys are right. I know we talked about this before 5th grade ended and I'm not holding up my end, that's on me.

I'm sorry that I'm not going to the same school as you guys, I promise I'll beg my mom to let me be with you guys. I will change. I promise. Just don't leave me. You guys are all the friends I have." I love you guys. Don't leave me."

Five minutes pass by as I watch the gray bubbles pop up back and forth, till finally a sentence replaced them.

"We're sorry Arri…You'll be okay."

The messages then turned blank. Blank because they were really gone and deleted my number forgetting my existence? Or blank because I chose to see it that way. Chose to turn off the part of my brain that hurted so much from reading the messages? That at any point any type of delusion could settle in and I would take it because it'd be better than facing the truth?

"You will be okay."

"You will be okay."

"You will be okay."

Those 4 words stuck with them with every second that passed by. I was sad. I was confused. Who were they to tell me that I would be okay? Who were they to decide that I was no longer essential to their lives, that I held no more importance? My confusion and sadness turned into anger and resentment.

I resented myself. Looking in the bathroom mirror in shame. How could I let this happen? Why was I so unlovable? Such a burden. Why was I feeling like this? I was a happy, care- free kid… wasn't I?

The blood in the body rushed to my face and arms. I felt hot and crowded. I needed to cool down. I needed to breathe but it was like I couldn't. It was like someone was slowly taking away my oxygen. Inching it farther and farther away.

I went into my room, I could no longer bear the smell of disappointment and failure coming from the bathroom. I grabbed my notebook and a pencil. Trying to distract my mind any way I could. I flipped to the nearest blank page. The ink quickly filled the white surface, stroke by stroke. Poetry began to spill in twisted tongues, using only words that my mind allowed in. Only words I would understand.

You yell you hate me but whisper you love me, I'm confused

You tell me I make you happy but when I come around you're unamused

You said it was forever, and shame on me because I believed

You said It would always be us, that three was the key

I was betrayed, twice in a row

I was hurt, by the people I loved most

My heart feels-

Snap

My pencil broke and those voices that I was able to silence by the sound of my pencil gliding each line soon came to an end. I jumped up and quickly looked for a new pencil. My pencil box was a mess, I mean considering that I haven't cleaned it since school got out it was a reasonable mess... But still pretty gross. I still went through it hoping to find a crayon or something that was in one piece. Anything that could do, anything to silence those voices again but instead I found a halfway broken pencil sharpener. Getting tired of searching for another pencil, I grabbed the pencil sharpener and my broken pencil and headed to the bathroom to sharpen my pencil over the trash can.

As I walked into the bathroom door my grandma let the dogs back in the house from being outside all day. I never understood why we just didn't install a doggy door but I guess it would be unnecessary since every time the dogs have to go they just let us know anyway. They were rowdy as usual but my dog princess must've been super excited to see me for some reason because immediately after she let her in, she came and jumped on my legs.. causing me to drop my already broken pencil and halfway broken sharper that already had old sharpening in it. Great. It was like bad things after bad things kept happening. Like the world wanted me to lose my mind. I picked up all the old sharpening that sat on the floor and the plastic shelling that protected the blade and threw them away. The blade though had disconnected from the plastic covering and was on the floor. I never knew that it could do that. I mean I knew that the blade was in there, how else would the pencil get sharp but I thought that it came with the plastic. Like it was forever stuff in there.

I stared at the blade lying on the floor. I wanted to pick it up and throw it away with the rest of the sharper but for some reason I was stuck. Like my body was refusing to pick up the blade and my eyes just kept staring at it. Staring at how sharp it was. It wasn't like a knife sharp but like a paper cutter sharp. The type that slices each paper to precision, leaving nothing but the exact line it was made to create. Or the type of knife that made cutting steak so easy. That could make any cut easy and painless.

Stop. That's not me. I wasn't some girl that would shed my own blood and let it be wasted. I grew up being taught that blood was precious. That being alive was a gift that not all can cherish. That it was beautiful and shouldn't be wasted. It was given to you by your parents and god and that they blessed you with the means to live.. But what if It was just a little.

Like a paintbrush waiting to paint its canvas with the right color. What if I brushed so lightly that barely any paint came out. I mean it would focus the pain on something else. That is to say when I got a paper cut all I would do was focus on the cut and how to not get any hand sanitizer in it. Sometimes I would even forget to do my chores because I was so focused on making sure the band aid was tight enough so that no cleaning products would get into it… What if it was like that? A couple months before school got out a counselor visited our class and told us how middle school can be scary and hard and how you might lose or gain friends. How some kids tend to get really sad and how the school has resources for those situations, but I wasn't even in middle school yet and it was already happening to me. What if middle school is ten times harder? I can't handle this pain again.

Finally, I was able to move again. My legs moved towards the blade and in my hands it appeared. I turned and looked at the trashcan. Contemplating my decisions.

" It'll be fast", I told myself.

"I won't even be able to see the cut, I'll be careful."

"I'll be careful."

"I just need the pain to be focused on something else, that's not bad."

"It's just a little distraction, I tell myself. Everyone deserves a distraction from time to time, it's healthy. Just a little distraction. It was like California. That's all. That's it."

I lifted the paintbrush over my wrist. My hands shaking but my mind clear. The first stroke was light and guided. It was like nothing happened. It felt bare. I stroked the paintbrush again. This time I felt a little sting. It was like a push almost. Like the first brush wasn't enough but this time was perfect. This time I felt something. The pain began to focus on my left arm. I felt relieved. It was like a hot soda on a Sunday day, waiting to be open because all the pressure had built up to the top. My skin began to paint the line I drew with the paintbrush.

"Just one more." I told myself. The last stroke just felt right and relieved so much pain, one more can take the rest away.

One more stroke, turned into two more and then three and next thing I know.

My silver paint brush had covered my entire canvas cherry red leaving no more room for white.

CHAPTER 7

Middle School

I cleaned up after myself and tucked the blade away in my underwear drawer. It worked. It was done. All the pain I felt in my heart was gone. I quickly showered after, cleaning off the paint. It burned as I showered. I kept my left arm out of the water, trying to not get any soap in it. I thought that could cause an infection and I don't need anything else going wrong and I for sure didn't need my parents to think I was some sad kid who needed help because I didn't. It was a one-time thing and it helped, really. I didn't even think about anything regarding 5th grade for the rest of the night. I was numb. I dried off and went to bed. I slept peacefully, almost feeling like I was floating. I haven't slept like that in such a long time. Maybe it was the relaxed feeling of the shower, or the fact that I felt so relieved and at ease.

The following week I got dressed and ready for student orientation. I haven't had anything to look forward to since my art day.

I liked to call it that instead. It makes it sound more positive and less "sick". I wasn't sick, I didn't need help or medicine or anything like that... I just needed a little breather.

The first day of middle school was in 3 days and I was determined to let the past stay in the past. I was going to be better for myself and for my new friends in the future. I already knew what not to do. I wrote it all down in my journal.

1- Don't mention anything smart and nerdy

2- Working out is lame. Act like a girl!

3- Dress more upbeat, whatever everyone's wearing, match it

4- AND MOST IMPORTANTLY ALWAYS BE AVAILABLE AND DO ANYTHING YOUR FRIENDS WANT OR NEED YOU TO DO!

I was going to be a 6th grader; these rules were mandatory. Eat, sleep and breathe them so I can have the best easygoing year ever. No more thinking about elementary school or my friends from the past. I'm going to be a whole new me!

"Hey Arri and Monney, are you guys ready to go?" My mom calls from the kitchen. My sister was coming because she was going into the 4th grade and wanted to see what a middle school looked like up close, I suppose. I was kind of surprised when she said she wanted to come, the orientation was at 9am. If you know anything about my sister from this whole summer, you know that she is not a morning person at all. She values every little bit of sleep she can get.

"Yes." we say in unison.

The school was big and open. In elementary school we had a whole bunch of hallways inside the building and just the playground and P.E outside but in middle school some of the hallways were outside, like the actual classes and stuff. They were right by the lunchroom. It was odd. So different... but nothing compared to what I found out next...

"NO PLAYGROUND??" I scream to my mom as I overhear some kids talking about how they're going to miss recess.

"Haha, no darling." My mom giggles.

"You only get recess from k-5th, after that you never get it again."

I stare at mom with my mouth wide. No one wanted to tell me this before I decided to graduate? I could've held myself back. Yeah I would've been in class with the old 4th graders but at least I would've had time to set the new monkey bar record. I bet there's someone waiting to hang on the bars longer than 57 seconds and take my place as the school champion. I can't believe this.

"Hey babe, you don't want to take off your hoodie? It's hot in here." asked my mom.

"Uh no, I'm fine. Thanks though." I say turning away from her and clenching my wrist.

"Never again." I whispered to myself as I looked at the lady who was about to speak.

"Hello students! We are so glad to have you here with us this morning. I am extremely happy to say in 3 days you will officially be a bighorn!!

I thought that being a "bighorn" meant that one of us had to dress up like the school mascot and go to all the school's events and parades, but my mom said that only happens in the movies. I wouldn't have minded it though. As long as I was able to run through the crowd at the games and start the wave, I would've been fine.

"Everyone please grab one of the white sheets of paper and head over to the left side of the cafeteria." the lady with the blonde hair announced. I think she was one of the counselors there.

My mom grabbed my white paper for me as we all walked over to the far side of the cafeteria. It was so big and so different. In 5th grade we had a big lunchroom don't get me wrong, but not as big as this. The ceilings even stood high, forming a triangle at the point. My old cafeteria only had a flat ceiling.

The lady started going over what we should expect the first couple weeks as bighorns, how to open up our lockers, how many classes we have a day and how to stay calm if we ever feel overwhelmed. She said that we had a social services provider there to always make sure we are safe... I wasn't sure why we needed that. If you don't feel safe, don't you just call the police? But I digress.

For the rest of the time, we got to walk around the school and go to the classrooms of our teachers. I had 6 whole different teachers. One for each subject. I had science, math, pe, English, dance and social studies. My favorite teacher was definitely my science teacher. Mrs. Schutze. She was the funniest teacher ever, well from the 10 minutes I spent in her class. You could tell she was just a sweetheart who truly loved her job. My mom said people like that are rare to find. The ones that love what they do and who they help more than the reward they get from it and I couldn't agree more.

We spent around a little over an hour at the oration and then headed home. My sister couldn't stop talking about how she's going to enjoy every moment on the monkey bars now. I rolled my eyes wishing that I could still have monkey bars but it was okay. I was getting something better. The opportunity to grow and change and find myself or who people want me to be. Same thing.

It felt like the next three days went by so slowly. I was counting the minutes until my first day of middle school. I pick at least 10 different outfits every day, trying to find the perfect one. Skirt and a crewneck? Eh too dressed up. Jeans and a hoodie? Ugh, too dressed down... but thankfully I found the perfect outfit right in time for the first day of school!

Chapter 8

Is This Real

"Get up Get up, ooouuu..... Get up Get up." My alarm went off.

Okay. listen. I know my alarm seems kind of odd but it got me up and ready to be in the best mood every time I listened to it and that was exactly what I needed today soo hush.

I woke up and went to the bathroom. I saw this YouTube video that said if you say positive things about yourself in the mirror when you first get up you'll believe it all day.

"I am beautiful."

"I am smart."

"I am kind."

"And I am enough" ... I say pushing back my bracelets on my arm and feeling the scars on my wrist. It's been almost a week or so since… yeah… and they're healing well. I started to put Neosporin and cocoa butter on them to help the scaring. That's what my mom would do when I would get hurt running on the blacktop in elementary. The bracelets were to cover up my art. I didn't want anyone thinking that I was "insane" or something. I didn't wanna become this label…

After I finished brushing my teeth and washing my face I put on my outfit. Ah, I was so excited. I had picked out my pretty baby blue jeans with my bright pink shirt and my pink Jordan 11's. The cutest outfit ever!

Okay so now I had the cutest outfit on, it was time to pack my lunch. My grandma used to pack my lunch but she says since I'm in middle school now I have to pack my own. I didn't really complain about it though because that just meant I could bring more snacks for lunch without any hassle. I had to make sure I packed two of everything. Two cookies, Two Lunchables with the caprisins on the side and two oranges, Just in case anyone asked for some. I heard that food is a good way into anyone's heart, well in my case friendship.

After I packed my lunch, I waited on the couch and watched tv, anxiously waiting to leave. After a good fifteen minutes of paw patrol, and five minutes of pacing back and forth, it was finally time to leave.

The drive was kind of far. I'd say a good fifteen minutes. My old school was right down the street from us, it was so close that mom would even let us get some extra time to sleep in if we already had our outfits and lunches packed the night before.

I arrived at the school and my heart began to race. I couldn't tell if I was excited or nervous. I think my mom could tell though because she started telling me all these positive things.

"Hey, remember that I love you so much and you're going to be fine. I know it's scary because you don't go to school with your sister anymore so, if you need anything don't hesitate to call me. Make sure to listen to your teachers and eat all your lunch!"

"Okay mom, I love you too." I said back to her as I opened the car door and started to head into the school. For some reason it looked different than it did at orientation. Maybe because there were hundreds of bodies that were in the school now.

From eleven years olds to fourteen years olds. All in the same building. I mean yeah it was the same thing in elementary school but we were all kids and now we're kids mixed with teenagers. It's different. You can't do certain things or you'll be labeled as "childish" or "immature."

My mom dropped me off early so I could get familiar with my locker before my classes started. Our middle school started at 8:00 on the dot, so I got there at 7:45. My locker was in the middle row of the quad. We had three rows that had some pretty decent space in between them. Unfortunately, though, we weren't able to buy our own locks for safety purposes; so, I had to remember my combination. I was pretty good at remembering things anyways, so it was alright. I didn't mind.

My locker number was 0878 and my code was 2:26:34. The most random numbers there could be... now remember when I said I was good at remembering stuff ?... I would like to disregard that.

I couldn't remember my combination for the life of me. It was as if every time I got it right and opened it up a few seconds later it was like I didn't even open it. I don't know but it was surely frustrating and that wasn't even the worst of it. I guess on the first day of school the bell rings five minutes earlier so kids can have more time to find their classes and guess who wasn't made aware of that... ME. So mid me trying to open my locker the bell rings and everyone starts finding their classes, meanwhile I have half of my stuff in my locker because I wanted to see if they would fit and now, I was late to class.

Of course, on the first day this happens to me. One of the administrators eventually saw me struggling and helped me open it. It didn't take too long but long enough to where I was going to walk into the class late and everyone was going to be staring at me.. What a way to start off the first day. Thankfully when I walked in everyone was still standing around and talking to each other. My first class of the day was science.

Before I sat down, I took a look around the room. "Mrs. S" the board read in big, bold, orange letters. She seemed very... what's the word...? Colorful. I already knew she was funny but the day of orientation, there was nothing in her room.

Her walls were decorated in all the colors of the rainbow. Her chair where she sat down at her desk had a fake fart pillow on it and the walls were decorated in funny science memes and encouraging cat posters. She was... perfect! All this plus that sense of humor that I mentioned earlier? Oh yeah, this was my jam. My kind of teacher honestly. I loved how creative and open she was.

"Hi students! I hope everyone is having an excellent morning so far! Please choose a seat. You may sit wherever you want besides the back row by Barry."

I continued to tour the classroom and came across the thing in the back that she wanted us to be cautious of.

It was a lizard? Well at least I think it was. It kind of looked like a baby alligator or crocodile. The rest of the class ran away at first glance at Barry, but for some reason I couldn't help but stare at him. He was so fascinating yet scary at the same time.

"Okay class, settle down, settle down. I am Mrs. S for the ones who didn't read the bright letter on the board... and I am your science teacher for the year! I am so excited to learn and push you all to your fullest potential."

The class sat in silence as Mrs. S gave all her energy to introduce herself. Part of me wanted to engage with her, let her know I was listening to her but the rest of the class didn't and I was sticking to my 3 rules of a successful sixth grade year. I did hold contact with her though and brought out a smile every now and then when she told one of her unfunny mom jokes, just to let her know someone cared.

"So I can tell everyone still needs a little bit of a wake up so we're going to play a game called icebreaker!"

Ou, I love icebreakers. It's a way you can make friends and connections without even knowing it. Okay well it all depends if someone finds what you do interesting or what you like interesting. You go around the group and say your name, favorite color and some interesting facts about you. It's supposed to help break the tension in the room but I think for my class it did the opposite.

"Okay class, who wants to go first?" Asks Mrs. S. Everyone sat there in silence staring at her with this blank stare.

"Okay... I can tell we have some shy kiddos around and that's okay. I'll just pull from the jar of popsicle sticks."

Every kid's eyes in the classroom lit up as soon as she said that. Everyone that once was a kid or currently is a kid KNOWS how terrifying the popsicle jar was. You never knew when it would be your turn to speak, you just knew that as soon as the stick with your desk number was on it that it was game over and you HAD to talk. See me I would rather volunteer and get it over with than have my stick pulled but no one seemed to raise their hand so I didn't either.

"Okay, desk number 19." called out Mrs. S. It was the desk that was closest to the rainbow wall.

"Um well hi, I guess. My name is Haley L Jane. The L stands for lora and my favorite color is baby pink, not hot pink though because that's yucky…Obviously. Umm I love golfing. I go with my parents to the country club every weekend, unless I'm out at the penthouse then I have to stay home unfortunately, but um yeah. Okay I'm done or whatever."

Haley's presentation was very, well, fun! She had a lot of really cool things to show off. Everyone was oohing and awing after her icebreaker. I'm kind of glad I didn't go first. I was just going to say that I love English and learning anything in general; Well maybe besides math. I was never too good at math even after the summer, but I loved English. Uhh I was going to mention Princess and how I was hoping to make new friends… but now that seems unornamented and tedious. No, I had to make mine more interesting and worth listening to. Maybe I won't mention the friend thing either, it does seem kind of desperate, so I'll hold off on it.

"Thank you so much Haley! Okay, who's next.. umm… Oh! Desk 12!" I look down at my desk and read my number. 12. Well, thank goodness I had some time to prepare. It was better to be second than first.

"Hello everyone, my name is Arrionna. Um, I love learning stuff. Well I love learning anything besides math aha. I love my dog Princess; she's a sweetheart and I love fresh veggies and fruit platters. Oh and on my weekends I like to run the track and read my books.'

Okay, so I don't know why I said that. It sounded like nothing I had planned. Well I had planned the first part, you know the name and learning thing but everything else was uncalled for.

I looked around the class and saw a bunch of blank stares. Not the same "Ou and "Aw" looks that Haley L. Jane got. I sat back down embarrassed.

"Well thank you Arrionna, I also love fruit and veggies!" Mrs. S announced. Well at least Mrs. S agreed with me! I mean she was pretty cool anyways so that made my morning feel a little bit better.

We did a few more icebreakers, went around the room and learned more about each other. After we did that for a little bit Mrs. S stopped and made an announcement.

"Okay class, now that we got to learn each other a little bit more, I think it's time you guys learn a little about me. As you guys all heard and saw, we have a friend here with us today." Mrs. S said pointing to the back of the classroom. She must've been talking about Barry the baby crocodile, or whatever it is.

"No he's not a weird looking snake or a baby crocodile... (she definitely had to be reading my mind when she said that)... but he is a bearded dragon!

Um, what now? Soo we have a pet dragon just sitting in the back of our classroom? Oh ok! Time for me to switch science classes.

"I was thinking, since this is an honor science class; Why not have mother nature right here with us. A beautiful understudied reptile. And with you guys being honor kids,

I trust we will treat Barry with some love and respect." Mrs. S continued.

She kind of had a good point, especially if she meant what she said about us being able to really study it. And honestly, that thing was pretty cute.

You know, once you look past all the scales and slime and stuff.

Anyways the rest of the class was filled with regular preteen discussion around the room and a little bit of what to expect for the semester.

Chapter 9

Am I Done Yet?

The rest of the school day was filled with the same things as science, besides the dragon part. Icebreakers and getting to know our teacher and the agenda for the year.

Math was the only difficult class I had so far. Every other class had a challenge presented somewhere, don't get me wrong, but math was different. When I was in math it was like I was an exchange student in a foreign country where no one speaks English and keeps trying to make me understand their language.

Now you might be like "Hey Arri did all those classes and tutoring this summer not help?" And yes, you do have a point but to be fair the touting was for the things I couldn't understand in 5th grade, not 6th and now that I look back at it I have no clue why my dad signed me up for that. But you know the past is the past.

I was in all honor classes, so I expected my workload to be more advanced and harder but just not as hard as math was. I wasn't too nervous though, I never gave up and regardless of this summer, I was good at challenges. Plus this year will be stronger, better, and happier! That I promised myself.

When I got home that day my mom had made dinner and asked us about our day.

"So, what was everyone's favorite point of the day?"

"Well, my favorite part of the day was when my teachers gave us 10 extra minutes of recess because we did good on our test today!" Shouts Monney.

"You had a test on the first day of school??" I exclaimed

"Well, it was one of those pre-tests that you can't really get a grade for but she said if we all got at least 20 out of 25 of the multiplication tables right then we would get extra recess."

"Well, that's good darling, and what about you Arri?"

"Um, well my day was pretty chill, the teachers just mainly did mini-introductions and let us have a free day for the rest of the class. I think it was because it was the first day, those days are usually pretty chill but I think my favorite part of the day was seeing a dragon in real life. It was pretty cool, my science teacher even said we can do assignments on it and get to learn about it."

"WHAT, NO WAY!" Monney shouts.

"How does Arri get to play with dragons and stuff? I want to go to middle school now."

"Well Monney, it's not an actual dragon. It is like a lizard; it's like the cousins to snakes." My mom explains to my sister.

"Ohhh, EW! Never mind I want to stay in 4th grade with my free recess."

We all laughed and continued to eat dinner. My mom had made fried chicken, white rice and asparagus. All my favorites. One big trait about my mom is that she knows how to cook really well. One time she made these homemade enchiladas, and oh my. Let's just say we didn't even leave any room for leftovers.

Anyways, my mom made Monney and I clean up the table and wipe down the counters before we went to bed.

The next few weeks of school were good. I was really starting to get a grasp of what middle school life was about. My classes level of intensity started to ramp up but that was all.

"Okay class, now that we're in the 5th week of school and you guys have been taking on every challenge, I threw your way without complaint... I am happy to announce that I have set up a field trip to the Spring Preserve where we can study all types of animals and even see more bearded Dragons!" Mrs. S said

Yes!! I was so excited! I didn't know what the Spring Preserve was fully but I did know that it had a bunch of animals that I loved and a free get out of school for the whole day card? Count me in!

I counted down the hours on the clock until 2:11, aka time to go home. I couldn't wait to show my mom the permission slip to go to the Springs Preserve! The last five weeks have been so boring and serious. This was going to be my time to show everyone the true and relaxed Arri and even possibly make some friends in my class, because I still haven't done that yet.

"Hiiiiii mom." I say as I buss open the car door.

"Well, hi there honey, how was school?"

"I mean it was good, in dance today we learned how to do a leap! You would think it was easy right? Oh, just jump in the air and keep your toes pointed but no! It's actually way more complicated than that, you have to make sure your-"

Okay that was a thing I do a lot. I can be so focused on one topic but then get distracted by another and go on about one thing for hours and then change the subject and go one about another for more… I don't know. My mom says it's because I just have so much to say that my mind doesn't really understand how long I can talk for. Maybe that's why I keep a journal. Without that I can just imagine how long I could talk for. Anyways back to the subject at hand

"And mom there is this field trip to this place called the Spring Preserve that my teacher is holding for my science class. They have all different types of animals and lizards and we can study them and-"

"Does this statement end with you asking me to please sign your permission slip so you can attend the field trip?"

"Um, well when you put it like that, yes." I respond fearsome, not knowing what she will say

"Haha, yes of course you can go. I'll sign it when we get home.

"YAY, THANK YOU THANK YOU!"

As soon as we got home, I started to plan my outfit. I had to wear something cute that screamed "Arri!" or at least something that would make people want to be my friend. I had 4 days to pick out my outfit so I wasn't stressing too bad. The field trip wasn't until Friday so I just had to get through the rest of the week which wasn't that long and with how long schools have been, I was definitely looking forward to this. And next thing I knew it was Friday!

Get up, Get up, ouuuu

My alarm went off. Yes. Finally. I got up a little bit earlier than usual so I could make sure I looked perfect. I put on my blue skinny jeans with my pink and yellow Steven Universe shirt and My black cardigan.

I loved Steven's Universe so much; I could talk about it all day. That's why I decided to wear it. All my cousins like it too, so it would be a great conversation starter for future longtime friends! I quickly grabbed my backpack and headed to the kitchen. Mom was in there making her morning coffee, the smell of fresh brew filling the air. She looked up when she saw me come in, offering me a bright smile.

"Good morning, sweetie! You look great today," she said, her eyes scanning my outfit. "Field trip day, right?"

I nodded, a big smile spreading across my face. "Yeah, I'm so excited! I can't wait. I think this is going to be the best day ever."

"I'm sure it will be. Hey, I got you something to get you going this morning." She reached into a bag and pulled out a Starbucks cup with a green straw. "I thought you might need a little pick-me-up before the big trip."

My eyes widened. "No way! You got me Starbucks?"

Mom chuckled. "Yep, I figured a little treat would help make your day even better. You'll need the energy. "I took the cup from her, my heart warming. The icy cold Frappuccino inside was the perfect start to the morning. "Thanks, Mom! You're the best." She smiled, a little bit of pride in her eyes. "You're welcome, honey. Have fun on your field trip, and remember to be safe. Call me if you need anything. Grandma is going to take you today because I have to go to work early today."

"Okay, bye love you!"

I quickly grabbed a granola bar from the counter, took a long sip of my Frappuccino, and rushed out the door. The caffeine already felt like it was hitting me, and I could feel the excitement building in my chest as I hopped into the car.

When I arrived at school, I was practically bouncing off the walls with anticipation or maybe with caffeine rush but you know. I could barely focus. All I could think about was the field trip. Finally, the bell rang, signaling the start of the day.

"Okay class, who's all ready for the field trip?" joyfully asked Mrs. S. The whole class screamed and jumped in excitement.

"Okay, okay settle down settles down. We will be departing shortly from the back of the school. We just have to give all the late straddlers a grace period of fifteen minutes then off we go.

I was so excited that the fifteen minutes felt like fifteen hours, or okay more like maybe 30 minutes but you get the point. The point was I was going to have the best day ever.

"Okay, are you guys ready? Everyone head to the back of the quad by the double doors and wait for the bus driver to give you permission to start boarding the bus. Please"

"Okay Mrs. S." We all said in unison.

I quickly packed up my stuff and fixed my necklace, waiting in the line to walk out the door.

"Hiiii, Airanna? isn't it?" says Haley

Omg. Haley was talking to me. Haley L Jane. Just the coolest girl in my class. You know, no big deal. Apparently she invited five girls from the whole school to go with her to the country house to golf. I wish I was one of those five but maybe now I can be. All thanks to my friend magnet of a shirt!

"Yeah, it's Arrionna." I responded back nervously.

"Ohh okay! Wait, that's such a cute shirt, where did you purchase it from."

"You think so?? My mom got it for me, I'm not sure where but I can ask her for you." I replied back.

"Um duhhh, yes ask for me. Hey, so like none of my friends are here so would you like to hang out with me all day?"

"Yes of course!"

"Okay great!"

I can't believe that Haley just asked me to hang out with her for the wholeee day. I mean yeah it was just because her friends weren't here today but that's okay because then I can become one of those friends and that's all I wanted. Just like I said, today was going to be a great day!

Chapter 10

Spring Preserve

    The bus ride to the spring preserve wasn't that long. I think we were only on the bus for about thirty minutes. Haley and I sat in the very front so we could see how the preserve looked as a whole. It was beautiful. Plants hung gracefully towards the walkway to the entrance. The sign was this bright, seasonal fall orange, with white letters dancing in the sun. And you could even see some of the animals' habitats from outside the gates.

    "Okay class, listen up. When we get off the bus there will be a tour guide who will guide us through the park and educate us on the creatures living there. No one is to interrupt her while she's talking, touch any of the animals without permission, and lastly wander off without an adult or at all for that matter. We will collectively have bathroom breaks and a lunchtime. Understood?"

    We all shook our heads yes to let Mrs. S know that we understood her rules and guidelines. After the preserve radioed the bus giving us permission to enter, we got off.

    The inside of the preserve was even better than the outside. It was like we were all explorers in the rainforest searching for the long-lost treasure that was mentioned in some old folktale from decades ago. The ceilings were very tall and open, giving an endless amount of room for the habitats.

"Okay boys and girls! My name is Erika and I'll be your tour guide today. I'll be showing you how things work, how we magnate all the animals we have and how they are fed and taken care of properly and lastly, I might even show you how to feed one today!"

Feed them? Oh, this day just keeps getting better and better by the second.

"Did she just say we would feed them? No way I'm putting my hand close to any type of smelly, nauseating creature!" Yells Haley.

"Well I don't think you have to, it was just an option." I replied, trying to keep her calm.

"Yeah, well you're not going to take that option right. I mean if you do that's okay, I'm not going to like to judge you or something but let me just say that would be like totally gross and unsanitary."

"Oh.. uh yeah that would be. Exactly why I'm not doing that. That's so odd." I say in reply to Haley's statement.

I mean I guess Haley had a point. You could catch any disease from letting an animal feed out of your hand. Then who would want to be friends with a sick girl who touches slimy animals. Even though I really wanted to feed one of them some snacks, I just left it alone. Haley is just trying to look out for what's best for me. Just like a true and honest friend would.

The first stop we took on the tour was by the tortoises. I had never seen a tortoise up and close before. I've seen them online and my grandparents did have a baby turtle that lived in the downstairs bathroom but not a tortoise. It was kind of weird though because when you would go to use the bathroom, he would swim on the other side of his tank just look at you. That was one of the reasons why I never really used the downstairs bathroom but I still loved the little guy.

"Okay guys, so this is Teddy the tortoise. He is about 20 years old. He's still a baby." says our tour guide

"He's a baby?" asked one of my classmates.

"Yes, he is, actually that's a great question. See, tortoises can live up to 80 years of age. They eat leaves, flowers and fruit and they don't eat meat.

I was surprised that they didn't eat meat. They have such big mouths but they also don't have any teeth, so they have to eat things that are easy for them to break down. It was kind of interesting actually, how even without something we think is so vile to our day-to-day existence they thrive and stay alive without it, while we probably would go insane.

Anyways hanging out with Haley was fun. We were mainly laughing about how slow the tortoises moved and picked which was our favorite, hoping they would race but they never did.. It's okay though, it was still enjoyable watching them in their environments. The day went by kind of fast but not fast enough. Our last stop will be the bearded dragon enclosure and that was the one I was most excited for but right now it was time for lunch and I was starving.

"What did you bring for lunch?" I asked Haley.

"Oh, my mom had just packed me some leftover lasagna, with asparagus and Milano cookies, I guess, it's alright. What about you? What did your mom pack you?" replied Haley.

"I got a Launchable, banana flavored applesauce, carrots and water." Banana applesauce was my favorite. It was like the two best fruits in one squishy pouch. Well, I actually don't really like apples but I like applesauce and apple juice. Even apple pie. I don't know why for some reason the actual fruit makes me nauseous. My mom says it's because the artificial taste sits better on my taste buds but I don't know.

"Oh. you eat those artificial applesauce packets?" Haley questioned

"Uh.. I mean only sometimes, just when I wanna cheat snack."

Was that not the right thing to say? I mean I liked the applesauce packets... I always did that's why my mom packed them but I guess it's something that's not "normalized". I'm not sure how to go about this. Was I to continue with my lie? Was I to act like I didn't like them and that my mom just put them in there? Or was I to tell the truth and risk Haley not wanting to be my friend anymore because eating artificial applesauce was disgusting and questionable?

"Oh, okay good! Had me worried for a second there, girl."

I guess I had my answer. I mean it was just applesauce. It wasn't anything too big of a fib. It wasn't like she was going to be with me all day every day, so I could just eat my artificial banana applesauce when I was at home. It was no big deal. We continued to eat lunch and watch the television show the Preserve had put on for us by the playground area. It was this discovery show of the wilderness. I wasn't really paying much attention.

"Haleyyyy!" someone screamed from the entrance.

"OMG MY GIRLSSSS!" yelled Haley as she ran up to 3 other girls who were in our class. Apparently, they all had woken up late and couldn't make it to the school to go on the bus so their parents dropped them off...

I didn't even know that was allowed, by hey at least now I can meet the rest of the friend group and they can get to know me. I opened my cardigan wide and made sure my bright pink and yellow Steven Universe shirt was showing and walked up to the rest of the girls.

Oh guys, this is ummm, wait so sorry tell me your name again." Haley asked me

"Oh it's okay, it's Arrionna but my friends call me Arri." I say back to the group

"Hii Arri." the girls said back

Okay that was a good sign, wasn't it? They called me Arri. They think of me as their friend obviously.

"This is Baylee, Crissy and Lily."

"Hi, guys!" I replied back

"Okay, well I think the next thing we're going to see is the ducks then the bearded dragons , so come on girls," said Haley

Haley and I threw away our lunch and followed the rest of the class to the main auditorium.

"Hi ladies, happy to see you three have joined us as well. So the next stop on today's trip is the Duck enclosure. Here at Springs Preserve we get our ducks pampered. Haha and no they're not literally wearing diapers, what I mean by that is that ducks are very attentive. They love to have the attention on them, to have every bit of food and engagement there is especially without their flocks. We like to make sure they are as comfortable as possible." Said Erika.

I did a report on marine life in 5th grade for our science fair and for some reason my teacher said to have ducks as a category... well I suppose that they can be "marine" but anyways I read that they don't really care for human attention unless they have food. But they probably get them when they are young from their mothers and raise them causing dependency. I wanted to ask to clarify it. It seemed interesting and intriguing. I raised my hand.

"I hope you're asking when we can leave this boring presentation." Haley says laughing with the girls.

"Aha, uh yeah I was going to just ask how much longer she was going to speak but it looks like she's almost done talking so I'll leave it alone." I say.

Um. okay. I didn't really know what to do. I liked learning. I like engaging and I sure didn't think anything about this field trip was boring. But I couldn't tell Haley that. The group would think it was weird. Apparently learning when you get into the 6th grade isn't something "cool". I was starting to learn that.

After a few minutes or so the tour of the ducks was over and we had fifteen minutes of free time in the auditorium to explore any animal that we wanted.

"Okay where do you guys want to go next?" I ask the group.

"Um well let's go to the bathroom first, I really have to pee. Mrs. S, may we go to the bathroom?" Haley asked

"Yes of course ladies, stay in a group and be back in ten minutes!"

The walk to the bathroom wasn't long. It was by the lunch area and the playground.

"Hey guys, after we're down here do you want to see the big fishes?" I ask

"Um yeah sure" said Lily

"After we hit this smoke of course." Haley said laughing.

"What?" I say in my head. There was no way what I heard was correct. I mean we were in sixth grade. We were eleven years old, Haley twelve. I can't believe that they were smoking. I didn't believe in that sort of thing. My parents didn't raise me to believe things like that were okay. They would kill me for even being friends with someone like this, for that matter I couldn't live with myself... but then what? I tell them how this isn't okay and we're too young to make life choices like this? How can it cause lifetime damage? I know I was new to sixth grade but I wasn't stupid. I know I would get called lame and a "teachers pet". I stood by the door and let them do their thing. Watching silently. After a few minutes of them passing around the electric smoker in silence. Crissy finally spoke.

"Okay guys, unfortunately we have to go back before they start coming to check on us or whatever."

Thank gosh. I never wanted to be out of a room so bad.

"Yeah, you're right, we need to leave... just as soon as our new friend Arri hits a puff!"

What. Did. She. Just. Say?

I can't. I won't.

"Oh no thanks, I'm okay thank you." I responded back fast but quiet

"Um, why not? Are you "too good" or something." asked Baylee.

"No, I didn't say that. I just don't want to and plus I think we should go."

"See, I knew she thought she was better than us. I mean she combines apples and bananas at one time. Btw it's not even cool, it's just weird. Just like your shirt. No one even knows what that is, first off. Only you. Only you would watch something weird and unheard of. You've tried so hard to be our friend and we gave you a chance and you blew it. So now have fun having no friends and have fun finding people that do the weird stuff that you do!!" screamed Haylee as she and the rest of girls walked away and bumped into me. And all of a sudden I was in the fifth grade all over again or would I say going into the start of the sixth grade all over again? People that I thought were my friends or at least pretended to be left me as soon as our interests didn't align. I mean I know that I'm young and that when I get older I'll find some "true" friends. I'll find people who love me for me and it won't hurt as bad if I bump into the wrong people. We'll be adults and we'll go about our ways in life, but if all this was happening now; at the age of 11... what would I deal with at the age of 21? I know that life isn't perfect. My mom tells me that we'll face trials and tribulations everyday but how many do I have to face before I get a break?

I overheard my grandma telling my aunt how "god gives his strongest soldiers the hardest battles" but why would he give us any battles if he loves us and wants us to be happy and joyful? I never understood it. Just as I'm not understanding things now. Tears started to roll down my face as I looked in the mirror and criticized my shirt.

"Why did I wear this shirt?" I thought to myself. I wanted to rip it off. I wanted to crawl out my own skin. I felt embarrassed and betrayed. My cardigan began to feel cold and lifeless as if it wasn't there to keep me warm anymore but to cover my scars that began to fade within my skin. To cover those moments of weakness I had weeks ago but still it felt like it just happened. What is wrong with me? Why am I weird? Why did I enjoy learning? Why couldn't I be like everyone else my age? Liking boys, going to sleepovers, wearing crop tops and skinny jeans, not dumb shirts from weird tv shows that no one bothered to watch. Why must my heart beat so loudly and so big for those whose hearts wouldn't even beat twice for me?

Those thoughts that once bombarded me weeks ago began to come back in a flash.

No. Not here and not again. This wasn't the way out for everything. I couldn't use this as an escape every time something got hard. I quickly rinsed my face and headed back with the rest of the class. When I got back we were already on to the bearded dragons. Since we already had experienced one in our class, we were allowed to touch them.

"Here you go sweetheart, hold your hands out with your palms up and he'll crawl out of my hands onto yours." Erika instructed. And that's what he did.

The little guy was so small but yet had the grip on a toddler. It was kind of strange. As soon as he got into my hands he just laid there staring up at me. He was adorable and definitely took my mind off of everything that happened. It was kind of funny though, they appear to be this thing that is labeled as "scary" or "intimidating" when in reality they are just so much more…like myself?

How I'm not "weird" just misunderstood by kids my age? Something along those lines, I'm not sure but I know tons of thoughts were going through my mind with nowhere to escape so as soon as I got home I wrote in my journal and showered.

September 4th, 2018

Dear diary, today was filled with a hundred words said and a thousand left unsaid. I don't know who I am or who I want to be. I'm not even sure if I like the things I like anymore or if I don't like the things I think aren't me.. I just know I didn't give up today and that's all that matters.

Chapter 11

I Don't Know

The next few months of school were hard. I mean I had good days but they always seemed to be followed by the constant reminder of loneliness. The winter formal was coming at the end of the month but I had no friends to go with so I wasn't going to go. My mom said to just be myself and the right people will come to me but what if the right people don't find me? How will I find them?

Ring Ring

My alarm went off for the 5th time this week. The same old repeating pattern but at least it was Friday.

"Hey girls, what do you guys think about going to the movies and watching the Adams Family?" my mom asked as my sister and I got ready to get in the car.

"Yeah, I would like that." my sister says.

"Me too!" I agree. I loved watching movies, especially suspenseful, thriller movies and my mom knew that. I think she could tell that I was going through a slump and wanted to help.

My first two periods of the day went by kind of fast. I didn't have science today unfortunately but I did have art because our dance classes were filling up and if you moved electives to make more room then you would get 3 free snacks from the student stand, so obviously I switched out.

"Okay class, today we are going to explore our inner lion." said Mrs. Balaski. She was an older Russian lady and most of the time spoke in tongues but I liked her. She was always so positive and fierce.

"I want everyone to draw up what they think their inner lion looks like. It could be metaphorical or realistic. Anything you guys want, ready… go!"

I had no clue what my inner lion would look like. I feel like it would be a bird of some sort, maybe because if I could have a superpower, it would be the ability to fly. Only because then I wouldn't have to wait in traffic everywhere I go and be able to cut all the lines.

"What's wrong honey, creativity is asleep at the door?" Mrs. Balasaki asked me as she looked at the whiteness that filled my paper.

"Yeah I guess, I just don't know what my lion would look like."

I didn't even know what inner me was like, how could I possibly know what strong inner me looked like.

"That's okay honey, sometimes creativity doesn't just appear. It has to be thought on. Think of a time where something made you strong when you felt so weak."

Well, I don't know, really. I could think of when I was the last one to stay on the trampoline out of everyone when it started raining but I don't think that really fits.

"Well I don't know." I sadly responded back

"Okay. what do you do when you feel sad or overwhelmed?"

"Um, well I write in my journal?"

"Okay, that's good. That's your lion. A book, A journal, that right there is your avenue, draw it!" Mrs. B says smiling and walking away. I grabbed the colored pencils and the markers from the box and started doodling away and before I knew it I was done. My lion was done.

"Okay class, times up, and crayons down. Who wants to present first?"

I look at the drawing on my paper in awe. Maybe this was it. This was the way I put myself "out there and allow the people who are meant to find me, find me.

"I'll go." I say pushing back my chair and standing up.

"My lion is a pen. I know how crazy that sentence may sound to you guys. It was even crazier in my head, but it is true. Our lions are described as something that makes us feel strong and protected. That makes challenges appear like tasks and for me, a pen is that. Anytime I feel like I can't handle the tough parts of growing up I write my way through it. Though it is mainly through my dairy, it helps. It makes all the bad thoughts and voices go away and for that it is my lion."

"Excellent job Arrionna! Everyone give Arriona a hand!"

That felt good. Unleashing what my inner "lion" was and saying it out loud.

"Hiii, I'm hazel." says this girl across from my table.

"Oh hi, I'm Arri."

"I know, I just wanted to say I enjoyed your presentation so much, I too always like to write when I get upset but mainly draw. I found that both are soothing and peaceful. I even drew a paint pallet for my inner lion."

"Oh wow, that's cool. I like that idea." I replied back to Hazel cautiously. Not getting too excited that someone was taking interest in me again. Considering what happened the last few times with friends, I'd rather take precautions.

"Yeah, maybe tomorrow at lunch we can hang out?" asked hazel.

"Yeah, sure." I replied.

My excitement grew just a smudge. Hazel seemed genuine and good. She even likes the things that I like. Maybe this could be a sign that things will start looking up from here but I made sure not to rush things.

The school day went by pretty fast, and well. I took home my drawing for my inner lion and showed my mom.

"Well that's beautiful baby, why won't you go hang it up on the fridge and we're going to get ready to go as soon as Monney get out of school.

Monney got out around an hour or so after me. I ended at 2:11 and she ended at 3:21 so I had time to relax and take off my shoes before we went to the movies.

"Are you hungry?" my grandma asked me.

"Um, no I think I'm going to eat at the movies but thank you." I respond.

"Oh you mommy and sissy are going to go to the movies?"

"Yeah we are going to go when Monney gets out of school."

"Mhm, nice to know I didn't get an invite." my grandma mumbled underneath her breath.

I pretended not to hear it and went on watching YouTube videos on my iPad. I had a good day so far and wasn't going to allow it to be ruined. I just couldn't wait to see the Adams Family in 3D with a massive slushie and popcorn.

My mom went to go pick up Monney and we headed out to AMC. It was our favorite movie center because of the big cup holders and reclining seats.

"Okay you guys can pick one candy. One that you guys agree on because you have to share."

Oh that was easy. Monney and I both loved the little airheads bites so we got those without hesitation. My mom even let us get our OWN large slushies and even refill them during the movies.

The movie was so good. It was just like the trailer and it wasn't too scary to where I wanted to take my glasses off and close my eyes but just the right amount of scary to where I was gasping at the main character's unforeseen actions. It was so refreshing. Today was already looking better than the days before, the months before... and I was nothing but grateful.

Chapter 12

Even Good Days Have to End

The ride back home was even better than the ride there. My mom had played all the best songs with the windows rolled down so we felt the fresh air in our faces.

"Okay I'm going to drop you guys off and then head to your aunt's house for a little bit and pick up dinner after." my mom told us.

"Okay mom, love you see you later."

Monney and I got in the house and watched some TV before she fell asleep. I don't understand how she went to bed without getting a late-night snack. It was mandatory for me to eat at least an orange or something before bed so off to the kitchen I went.

"What are you doing?" my grandma asked me

"Oh I'm just peeling my orange and getting ready for bed." I respond

"WHAT? Those aren't for you! They're for your grandfather Brandon." she yelled at me

"Oh, sorry I didn't know." I replied no longer peeling the orange and giving her my full attention.

"You just don't think at all Arrionna. Everything in the world doesn't revolve around you. Have you ever thought of that? You just go around and-"

My mind shut off. Was it my mind? Or ears? Or my sanity just slowly fading away. Not this again. I thought we stopped this months ago. I can't deal with this right now. I let her continue on and find my avenue to start talking again once my head can no longer detect her talking.

"I didn't know, I won't do it again. I'll just leave the orange in the fridge."

"No you won't! You won't waste that orange now! You should've never touched it now you're going to get me yelled at ."

"I said I didn't know, I just wanted a snack. Can you just stop?"

"Oh so now I have to shut up in my own home? God, you just make me want to kill myself, sometimes do you know that Arrionna?"

It's like the air stopped and every atom and molecule that was floating around disappeared and choked me up.

"Oh." I say to my grandma as I walk back into the room with my sister. Words couldn't explain the thoughts running through my head at that moment. I couldn't fathom the things she just said. All I wanted was an orange. I didn't know that those were anyone's. I didn't mean to get my grandma in trouble again by my grandpa. Those thoughts, the ones from months ago appeared once again. Clouding my mind. I grabbed my journal from the side of my dresser and took it into the bathroom and I slammed the door. Why was everything so hard? So confusing. So temperamental. I start off with a good day and it ends bad. I start off with a bad day and it ends bad, when does it stop? When can I go back to who I used to be in grade school? Back to the young girl who was happy. Who didn't have a problem in sight, I mean yeah, some days were hard but I had people to help me get over them and make it easier but now… now who do I have? My sister is too young to understand. She deserves to be happy and keep her peace, she doesn't need my problems put on her. My parents don't understand. All they say is how things will get better and how I don't even know the half of life yet but what if I didn't want to. What If I just wanted to know nothing anymore? Be aware of nothing? What if I didn't wanna be here anymore?

These questions clouded my mind every time I felt like I wasn't needed here or didn't belong. This was my pattern. The pattern I tried so hard to break but seemed to fall back to every time. I ran back into my room where my sister slept as my tears began to overflow. I grabbed the blade from the broken pencil sharpener and went back into the bathroom. I looked in the mirror and took a deep breath.

My skin started to feel hot again, overwhelmed by every emotion I was having. Unclear about each. Unclear about if this was what I really wanted or was it what I felt like I needed in the moment? I couldn't decide. All I knew was I wanted the pain to stop. I wanted to be able to breathe without life controlling each breath I took. I wanted... I needed...a break. I looked down at my wrist and traced my scars with my index finger.

"Just a few strokes." I murmured that familiar sentence to myself again. One more and that's it. Just until the pain goes away.

I held the silver blade over my wrist and began making art again. My paintbrush making thicker lines than the last time. Each brush against my skin felt so relieving, but not enough. I could still feel the pain.

Five more strokes I gave it and still, no difference. I turn my wrist more over to the left and look at the blue vein resting underneath my skin.

"If I just nick a small part of that then the pain will be gone. It'll hurt more than skin and then I'll be done." I thought to myself as I cried on the bathroom floor with my left wrist covered in bright red paint.

"Just one more stroke." I mumbled...

"Sorry baby, I have to pee so bad but grandmas toilet is out of tissue so can I just grab some-"

Chapter 13

My Parents

I dropped the blade on the bathroom floor as I froze seeing my mom open the door and stare at my wrists.

No. No, no, no, no, no. This wasn't how it was supposed to go. I was supposed to just ease the pain a little bit and go about the night. I didn't realize how quickly time was passing. I didn't realize how long I was in the bathroom.

My mom just stared at me. Her face flustered. I could see the tears forming in her eyes as she tried to hold them in. It felt like she stared for what could've been hours. She looked at the blade on the floor and picked it up.

"I'm going to get you a cold towel and some Neosporin. Clean up the blood, put it on, then head to bed, I'll get some more Band-Aids at the store tomorrow." my mom said, closing the door.

I was stunned. It felt like my reality wasn't real. Like I was in a different universe or something watching myself through a lens. My mom seemed traumatized. I could tell she didn't know what to do or say but just wished she never saw that. No mother should see that. What have I done?

I cleaned myself up, turned off the light and put the covers over my head. I wanted nothing more than to just fall asleep. I wanted to forget what happened. To forget the disappointment on my mother's face. I let her down. All my life she's taught me to be strong and endure through any crisis and look at me now. Painting my wrists to help me not feel anything. I had broken her number 1 rule. Never give up.

I eventually fell asleep in a puddle of my own tears, waking up with my eyes puffy and red and to the sound of my mother's voice.

"Wake up, Arrionna. Your dad is outside to see you."

I look over at my alarm clock and see the time. 3:04am.

"Huh?" I say. Barely grasping anything she's saying.

"Go by the front door and put some socks on. It's cold outside.

After 2 minutes or so I finally make it to the front door to see my father standing in between the doorway.

"Dad?" I ask

"Arri?" he says, but something sounded different than usual. His voice seemed… shaky.

"What's wrong, why are you here?" I ask him. Almost immediately my dad dropped to his knees and began crying.

"Please Arri, I love you so much. You are my everything. You saved my life when I had you. My first-born child. Please. Please, Please, Please. Don't try to leave me again. I need you.

And suddenly the "art" I was creating on my arm, appeared in its true form. It was no longer art but destruction. I was destroying myself. I was destroying my family.

I stared at my father and watched the tears run down his face as he looked at me. At that moment I realized how much I had. I realized I had a family who loved me. I didn't want to die anymore. I didn't want to leave my parents without their firstborn. I didn't want to abandon my sister. I didn't want to ever hurt my father like this again. Tears began to run from my eyes too. My dad grabbed me and just hugged me for what felt like hours. In silence we sat, comforting each other and wiping each other tears.

"I love you kid. I love you so much. We all love you and need you here with us. You matter to us" My dad told me, handing me a box of Band-Aids before he left. I could tell he didn't want to leave. His hands were shaking and his forehead was sweating. My dad. What did I do to my dad.

"I love you more." I whispered back to him.

I walked back into my room to see my sister and my mother awake sitting on the edge of the bed. I sat down next to them and almost immediately I was greeted with hugs and tears once again. My mom sat in silence. I could feel her rapid heartbeat on my shoulder as she tried to control her breathing. My sister stared at the ground with her head on my shoulder.

I can't remember when we went to sleep that night. It was all such a blur. I think we all fell asleep holding each other.

Chapter 14

I Survived

My life after that was still a challenge but I had the support I needed. I got help from my family. We had daily talks. We talked about the hardest points of my day and the easiest. About what I can do if I have those thoughts again and who I could come talk to. We talked about goals we had in life, and what we would do to accomplish them and at the end of every conversation they reminded me how much I was loved and how important I am. Some of my family even joined in on the talks and told me what they would do in my shoes, so I didn't feel like all the pressure was on me to talk. My parents had discussed my situation with some of the family, which was okay. I understood that they needed help in this, we all did. I stopped thinking about the consistent need for friends and entered my school's writing club. I found people there who loved the things I loved and understood me, though we didn't hang out every day and all day; they were still really cool people. I realized that a friend isn't someone who you hang out with every day or who likes the same things as you. A friend is someone you can count on, someone who won't judge you for you and most importantly someone who makes you feel like your life is worth living. They encourage you to be your best self and nothing less. Eventually I got through the year and just like everything else I still had my ups and downs. There were times where I still had thoughts to attempt. I would be lying if I said after that it stopped.

The truth is that recollection of those thoughts never just "go away". There are times where I'm cutting tomatoes for dinner and just think what if. "Just one more". But the truth was there was never going to just be "one more". If I kept cutting I would've never stopped. I would've just kept negotiating my life, until eventually there was no more to give and I was gone.

Sometimes on your happiest day you sit back and for that second of silence you remember. You remember the hard days. The days when you questioned who you were. The days that everyone doubted you. The days you contemplated the worth of your existence and that's okay but in the following moment, release yourself of those thoughts and correct them because no matter where you're at in your life. It is worth living. You are worth living. You are worth every atom of space you take up because God makes no mistakes, and he made you.

And so every time those thoughts come or my scars begin to brighten up or darken with the seasons, I remind myself just that. That I, Arrionna Wright-Cross, survived the world's deadly disease.

I survived depression.

Epilogue

I wrote this book to yeah, share my story, but to help people understand that this life we live is not easy. It doesn't matter if you're wealthy or poor. White or Black. Young or old. Life can hit you with anything at any time and sometimes it might just feel like it's too much. Like this life you're living isn't meant for you and that it would be better off without you. That no one understands the thoughts in your head or the pain you carry every day. It is a struggle to live. It is a struggle to survive. And it is so normalized to have this certain lifestyle that proves otherwise but I promise you it's not real. People who appear to have a perfect life with no worries and no stress, aren't real. You will not want to get up one day. One day, you will face a pain and hurt that feels unbearable. You will face trials and tribulations that will not feel worthy of life and I won't say that you'll bounce back better than ever and everything will be okay after because that's not true. Sometimes you don't bounce back. Sometimes the person who you once were becomes lost in all the chaos. Sometimes you become a different person. And sometimes that different person is harder to recognize, even by yourself. The changes are subtle at first, but they start to show up in the way you think, the way you feel, the way you react. You might become someone you didn't expect, someone you're not sure you even like. And that's okay, because it's part of the journey.

But here's the thing—just because things feel broken doesn't mean they can't be fixed. Just because you feel lost doesn't mean you can't find your way again. It's important to understand that even in your lowest moments, when everything feels impossible, you are still deserving of love, peace, and joy. Those dark days, the ones that make you question everything, will pass. They may leave scars, they may leave you questioning who you are or what your purpose is, but they will not define you. You get to decide that.

It's easy to feel alone in this world, especially when it feels like everyone else is living an easier, more perfect life. But trust me, nobody's life is perfect. We all have our battles. Some are just hidden better than others. The hardest thing is realizing that not everything is as it seems, and that's okay. It's okay to not have it all figured out. It's okay to not be okay sometimes.

The key is to keep going, even when the weight feels too much to carry. Reach out. Ask for help when you need it. You don't have to carry the burden alone. And don't be afraid to change along the way. Growth isn't a straight line. It's messy, it's confusing, and sometimes it feels like it's two steps forward, three steps back. But every step, even the setbacks, is progress. Every time you get up after a fall, you're showing yourself just how strong you are.

So, to anyone reading this, whether you're in the middle of your own storm or just starting to walk through it—know this: you are not alone. You are valid, you are enough, and this life, no matter how difficult, is still worth living.

About the Author

Hello! I'm a teen author—a term that feels a bit too formal for my taste. "Novelist" has a nice ring to it, though, as if to say, "Yeah, she's a novelist!" But in reality, I'm just a teenager who adores the color green, particularly sage. I seize every opportunity to dive into books and pen my own stories, all while embracing rainy days and epic car rides where the music blares through the speakers, drowning out any overthinking and worries.

Math often feels like an uphill battle for me, yet it somehow finds a way to challenge me time and again. And let's not even talk about how I can't watch movies without the subtitles—I swear I can barely hear out of my right ear! So, while "novelist" sounds impressive, I'm really just a young girl who loves to write.